T0311581

Reporting African Elections

The ability to be divided along ethnic and religious lines is inherent to much of Africa's media. Such potentially divisive reporting has the ability to incite violence through prejudiced information, particularly during election processes.

Reporting African Elections examines the impact of media messages on society, focusing on these electoral processes in Africa. Drawing upon the Peace Journalism approach to political reporting, this book offers a unifying conceptual framework for analysing the role journalists play in ensuring peaceful elections. Joseph Adebayo also looks at the impact training can have on election reportage, studying recent elections in Kenya and Nigeria in order to present a 17-point plan for reporting elections in Africa.

Reporting African Elections will be of interest to scholars and students of journalism, peace and conflict studies, and politics.

Joseph Adebayo is a postdoctoral researcher at the University of Cape Town. He holds a PhD in Public Administration (specialising in peace-building) from the Durban University of Technology.

Routledge African Studies

For a full list of available titles, please visit: https://www.routledge.
com/African-Studies/book-series/AFRSTUD

Reporting African Elections
Towards a Peace Journalism Approach

Joseph Adebayo

Routledge
Taylor & Francis Group

LONDON AND NEW YORK

First published 2019
by Routledge
2 Park Square, Milton Park, Abingdon, Oxon OX14 4RN

and by Routledge
52 Vanderbilt Avenue, New York, NY 10017

Routledge is an imprint of the Taylor & Francis Group, an informa business

First issued in paperback 2021

British Library Cataloguing-in-Publication Data
A catalogue record for this book is available from the British Library

Library of Congress Cataloging-in-Publication Data
Names: Adebayo, Joseph, author.
Title: Reporting African elections: towards a peace
journalism approach / Joseph Adebayo.
Description: New York, NY: Routledge, 2019. |
Series: Routledge African studies; 30 |
Includes bibliographical references and index. |
Identifiers: LCCN 2018048184 (print) | LCCN 2018049739 (ebook) |
ISBN 9780429427589 (Ebook) | ISBN 9780429764424 (Adobe Reader) |
ISBN 9780429764417 (Epub) | ISBN 9780429764400 (Mobipocket) |
ISBN 9781138384354 (hardback)
Subjects: LCSH: Elections—Press coverage—Africa. | Press and
politics—Africa. | Journalism—Political aspects—Africa. | Political
violence—Africa—Prevention.
Classification: LCC PN4751 (ebook) | LCC PN4751 .A34 2019 (print) |
DDC 070.4/4932496—dc23
LC record available at https://lccn.loc.gov/2018048184

ISBN: 978-1-138-38435-4 (hbk)
ISBN: 978-1-03-209417-5 (pbk)
ISBN: 978-0-429-42758-9 (ebk)

Typeset in Times New Roman
by codeMantra

Dedicated to Dr. Abduljeleel Gbemisola Animashawun,
my academic coach and mentor
and
Professor Geoff Thomas Harris, who supervised
my PhD thesis.

Contents

Illustrations

Figures

Tables

Foreword

Jake Lynch

"You don't leave bandits causing disorder. They are bandits, and they should be treated as bandits." So Paul Mangwana, the Zimbabwe African National Union–Patriotic Front (ZANU-PF) party spokesperson, told the *New York Times* (Moyo, 2018) as protests over the Zimbabwean election of 2018—the first since long-time president Robert Mugabe stepped down—turned violent. The same report quoted one of the demonstrators, Denis Chauke, an activist in his 20s and a supporter of the opposition Movement for Democratic Change Alliance: "If this fails, we will go physical. We will fight for our win."

What a win might mean, and what issues of concern had brought Mr Chauke and his colleagues on to the streets of Harare—at the risk of being labelled "bandits" and shot—remained obscure, at least to anyone relying on the *New York Times'* account. It was, in short, a familiar example of "War Journalism," as defined originally by Johan Galtung. This is to be distinguished from war reporting, meaning merely the reporting of wars, in any form. Rather, Galtung defines the mainstream of news, at least in commercial Western media, as likely to make violence seem inevitable, natural, even desirable. This is not the intention of editors or reporters, who typically set out—even in these days of fragmented mediascapes—with no other ambition than to report the facts as they see them. It is, of course, in the choice of those facts, and the influences brought to bear upon that choice, that issues with the news reporting of conflict, in any form, tend to inhere.

With co-author Mari Holmboe Ruge, Galtung published a landmark essay, "The Structure of Foreign News" (Galtung and Ruge, 1965), arguing that the chief influences on news content should be attributed to the structures—not only economic and organisational but also political and ideological—within which it was being gathered, reported, and disseminated. These gave rise to a dominant form in which violent incidents, with a negative effect on elites in elite countries, were most likely to be reported. Positive processes, benefiting non-elite people in non-elite countries, were least likely to be reported. Concentrate on events, at the expense of sequences of cause and effect leading up to—or potentially away from—such incidents, and you risk naturalising violence, even validating it as apparently the only possible recourse. Restrict newsgathering to elite, or official sources such as party spokespersons, and you might miss peace actions and initiatives underway at sub-elite levels. Stick to a surface narrative and you risk obscuring underlying issues, thus depriving those affected by them of the opportunity to express any form of dissatisfaction than by further violence.

In counter-position to this dominant form, Galtung (1998) proposed a remedial strategy that he called Peace Journalism. This would entail mapping multiple parties and enquiring into their goals; attending as much to grass-roots peacemakers as to those in positions of leadership; challenging propaganda issued by conflicting parties; and, last but not least, treating a conflict as a set of problems to be creatively solved, not a giant tug of war capable of being brought to an end only by total victory for one "side" over a sole "other." Iterated in the late 1990s, these ideas were taken up by journalistic communities digesting experiences—including considerable public criticism of their role—from conflicts including "Operation Desert Storm" in Iraq, in 1991, and the disintegration of federal Yugoslavia.

Peace Journalism quickly became an organising principle for programmes of media development aid, usually in the form of training and resourcing for professional journalists in societies affected by violent conflict (Lynch, 2007). Later, it began to be operationalised by scholarly researchers, typically by adapting the distinctions briefly sketched out above to different milieux of time and place, to derive evaluative criteria for content analysis. Pioneering studies in this category (such as Lee and Maslog, 2005) invariably showed some Peace Journalism was underway in the output of mainstream news organisations—thus sharpening the question, of how more could be fostered and brought about.

As more scholars developed an interest in Peace Journalism, this same process, of adapting the distinctions to "fit" the reporting of different stories, began to be extended beyond wars as such to other forms of conflict, including political violence. And so to the current volume by Joseph Olusegun Adebayo, which offers a comprehensive analysis of reporting by African media of elections in African countries, which have seen multiple incidents of violence associated with pre-electoral, electoral, and (as in Zimbabwe in 2018) post-electoral phases of democracy over the past several decades.

The study considers this troubling phenomenon through an extended consideration of a prominent example—the 2017 presidential election in Kenya, a country blighted by previous rounds of electoral violence that caused heads to be wagged in the conclaves of global governance. On this solid empirical foundation, a sophisticated theoretical approach is built up, to tackle one of its main research questions: Whether media should be seen merely as mediators, or also as instigators, of such violence. In answering such a question, of course, one must always allow for ill-intentioned actors which set out to provoke and foment unrest for their own purposes. The most notorious of these remains Radio Milles Collines, in Rwanda, which was implicated in the Genocide of 1994. But it is, perhaps, in cases where journalists unwittingly contribute to the conditions for violence, through their everyday routines and practices, that the main opportunities for reform and intervention are to be found.

Adebayo's other main contribution here is to adapt the Peace Journalism approach to fashion a practical and workable set of precepts, suitable for such journalists who wish to avoid becoming implicated in electoral violence and instead—in the standard field definition—provide their readers and audiences with opportunities to consider and value non-violent responses (Lynch and McGoldrick, 2005). One persistent criticism of Peace Journalism is that it asks journalists to do the impossible. Indeed, there is a paradox: The notion of Peace Journalism arose from a study whose signal contribution was to shift attribution of influence on news content towards the structures in which it was produced and away from the agency of individual journalists, and yet it has typically been applied in settings where individual journalists, being resourced with fresh ideas and approaches, are then expected to change the content of their reporting.

Here, Adebayo tackles this issue head-on by offering a fascinating annotated account of an "action research" project, involving journalists in Nigeria undergoing journalist training, before then undertaking the exacting task of reporting on a fraught electoral process in their country while avoiding the danger of becoming unwittingly complicit in any associated violence. The study culminates in the creation of an artefact that crystallises a good deal of high-grade scholarly labour, which will hopefully prove useful beyond the academy as well as within it: Namely an adaptation, to local purposes of covering elections in Africa, of a 17-point plan for Peace Journalism that Annabel McGoldrick and I first published in 2005. It is packed with useful and field-tested wisdom. To name but a few of its many salient points of advice: Look beyond the big cities, the party leaderships and their slogans, and the clash of personalities. Instead, seek out grass-roots activism, issue-based politics, and potential for common ground. This book represents a significant new chapter in the developing corpus of scholarly literature on Peace Journalism. It also sets forth an aspirational manifesto for journalists covering contested elections: One with rich applicability not only to African political and media actors but also to their counterparts in the rest of the world. It is truly a ground-breaking piece of work.

References

Galtung, Johan and Mari Holmboe Ruge (1965) "The Structure of Foreign News: the presentation of the Congo, Cuba and Cyprus crises in four Norwegian newspapers," *Journal of Peace Research*, 2 (1), 1965, pp. 64–91.

Galtung, Johan (1998) "High road, low road—charting the course for peace journalism," *Track Two*, vol. 7, no. 4, Centre for Conflict Resolution, South Africa.

Lee, Seow Ting and Crispin C Maslog (2005) "War or peace journalism in Asian newspapers," *Journal of Communication*, 55 (2), pp. 311–329.

Lynch, Jake and Annabel McGoldrick (2005) *Peace Journalism*. Stroud: Hawthorn Press.

Moyo, Joseph (2018) "Zimbabwe protests turn violent as some call election a sham," *New York Times*, August 2. Retrieved October 24, 2018 from: https://www.nytimes.com/2018/08/01/world/africa/zimbabwe-elections-protests.html

Acknowledgements

This book would not have seen the light of day without the vital contributions of many people, and I would like to sincerely thank them all. My gratitude goes to the hardworking team at the International Centre for Nonviolence at the Durban University of Technology (DUT), who gave me the opportunity, support, and confidence to undertake this research. Special thanks to Professor Geoff Thomas Harris, Dr. Sylvia Kaye, and Henson Crispin for their unflinching support.

I also want to specially acknowledge the funding and kind support I received from the National Research Foundation (NRF), as well as my colleagues and superiors at the Centre for African Studies, University of Cape Town. They afforded me the opportunity to collaborate with likeminded researchers and gave me the flexibility I needed to make the necessary trips to collect data on which this book relies. Special thanks to my principal investigator (PI) Professor Lungisile Ntsebeza for his guidance and fatherly advice, and to Ms. Noma-Afrika Maseti for enthusiastically providing all the logistic support I needed.

During my field trips to Nigeria and Kenya, I conducted interviews and gathered the materials used here, and I could never express enough gratitude to the journalists who provided all the information I needed. Special thanks to the Nigerian Union of Journalists (NUJ), Ilorin, Kwara State for providing all the necessary support for my field work in Northcentral Nigeria.

Special thanks to Dr. Christopher Ouma of the Department of English Literature, University of Cape Town for his invaluable tips and guidance.

I want to also sincerely acknowledge the warm support I got from the management and staff of Vida e Café, Rondebosch Main Road, Cape Town, where I wrote a substantial part of this book. Special thanks to my dear friends Robert and Emily Muller, as well as Mr. Paul Wakooba.

I say a huge thank you to my mentors Professor Jake Lynch and Annabel McGoldrick both of the Centre for Peace and Conflict Studies at the University of Sydney for their invaluable contributions to the success of this book. I especially want to thank them for granting me the permission to adapt their 17-point plan for Peace Journalism to this book.

Abbreviations

BBC	British Broadcasting Corporation
CDG	Centre for Democracy and Governance
CMS	Church Missionary Society
DRC	Democratic Republic of the Congo
EISA	Electoral Institute for Sustainable Democracy in Africa
EMBs	Electoral Management Bodies
ICG	International Crisis Group
IEBC	Independent Electoral and Boundaries Commission
JIC	Joint Intelligence Committee
MDC	Movement for Democratic Change
NASA	National Super Alliance
NATO	North Atlantic Treaty Organisation
NBS	National Broadcasting Service
NNDP	Nigerian National Democratic Party
NUJ	Nigerian Union of Journalists
ODM	Orange Democratic Movement
PJ	Peace Journalism
PJF	Peace Journalism Foundation
RTLM	Radio Télévision Libre des Mille Collines
WMD	Weapons of Mass Destruction
WNTV	Western Nigeria Television
ZANU-PF	Zimbabwe African National Union–Patriotic Front
ZEC	Zimbabwe Electoral Commission

1 Contextualising Peace Journalism

Introduction

With the exception of a few countries, election periods in Africa are usually anticipated with apprehension, because so often, they culminate in violence and bloodshed. Elections often turn violent in countries such as Nigeria, Kenya, the Democratic Republic of the Congo (DRC), Zimbabwe, and Burundi, where the governments are typically authoritarian, the people severely divided along ethnic and/or religious lines, and the management of political opposition is aggressive. In most African countries without a well-developed respect for the rights of citizens, elections increase political polarisation and potentially increase human rights abuses. Thus, electoral violence seems to be the norm rather than occasional occurrences in many African countries. In what can be regarded as an irony, Africa has witnessed more elections since the turn of the twentieth century. Sadly, the increase in elections has also resulted in increase in the number of electoral-motivated violence. It is imperative to note that electoral violence is not restricted to Africa alone, but the majority occur on the continent. For example, from 1960 to 2010, the world witnessed more than 350 unique cases of violent post-election protests, with most occurring in Africa.[1] Many factors can be adduced for the prevalence of electoral violence on the continent. For example, electoral violence is often perpetrated or instigated by both the incumbent in office and opposition elements. The incumbent, most times against the will of the people, wants to hold on tenaciously to power and avoid defeat, while opposition elements seek to wrestle power from the incumbent by all means, thereby wittingly or unwittingly instigating violence to the detriment of the society they claim to want to govern.[2] Electoral violence in Africa is also closely connected with the neo-patrimonial character of the African state, the nature of contestation for power, and the weak institutionalisation of democratic architectures, including political parties and electoral management bodies (EMBs).

One very important player in the political landscape of a society during the electoral process is the media. The media is a powerful tool of mass mobilisation—it is a two-edged sword, capable of motivating for peace or instigating violence. The relevance of the media in any polity is generally drawn from the fact that information is necessary for effective governance and administration, and the society depends profoundly on the media for vital information. This dependence by the public on the media gives the media immense influence—perhaps even in magnitude beyond the comprehension of media practitioners. For example, it can be argued that manoeuvre by the government of Burundi to clamp down on Radio Publique Africaine, and on all forms of media and communication—including Twitter, Facebook, Viber, and WhatsApp—for fear of disseminating information that will sensitise and mobilise the populace in the run-off to the contested general elections, is further proof of the government's realisation of the media's influence as a tool for mass mobilisation and sensitisation.

The onerous task of safeguarding and ensuring the transparency of the democratic process lies on the shoulders of the media. While society "sleeps," the media, like a watchdog, is expected to play an active role in ensuring that the electoral process is transparent. This is because transparency before, during, and after elections is required at all levels to ensure electoral integrity and foster peace before, during, and after the elections. The media [should] ensures that public gets access to information without struggle, that politicians are exposed and held accountable, that the legitimacy of individuals is ensured, and that it makes a case, through its reportage, that the public should be given the freedom to participate in debates without threats to their lives. The media can help in achieving all the aforementioned through deliberate reportage in ways that encourage non-violent civic participation.

Sadly, however, in so many elections—especially those held on the continent of Africa—the media has often been accused of inciting the public towards acts of violence through a style of reportage that lacks conflict sensitivity and that is not mindful of the sociocultural, sociopolitical, and religious differences that typify most African countries. Although it is very imprudent to adduce every electoral violence to the media, the role played by the media in the unfortunate 1994 genocide in Rwanda which led to the death of close to a million people, as well as the violent 2007 and 2011 elections in Kenya and Nigeria, and the violence that typified the 2013 Zimbabwean general elections readily comes to mind. These examples show a dire need to build the capacity of journalists across the continent to report sensitive social issues such as elections in ways that promote peace and not further broaden the already existing fault lines among Africa's very diverse and heterogeneous populace. This book makes a strong case for the adoption of the Peace Journalism (PJ) model as an "alternative" way of reporting elections on the continent. A sizeable part of the book reports a field study I conducted in Northcentral Nigeria while studying for my PhD. A detailed report of that study is presented in Chapter 5 of the book.

The growing wave of media-instigated violence and the need to channel the immense influence wielded by the media to promote social peace and harmony has given rise to the concept of PJ. Coined by Johan Galtung and popularised by Jake Lynch and Annabel McGoldrick, PJ is manifest when journalists deliberately make choices regarding the stories they report and the prominence they accord such stories, in ways that create opportunities for members of society to take the route of non-violence when responding to conflict-sensitive issues such as electoral tensions. PJ uses the concepts of balance, fairness, and accuracy to foster societal peace through the use of insights of conflict analysis and transformation.

This book explores the concept of PJ and how its application can help foster non-violent elections in Africa. Drawing from the examples of media-driven non-violent elections in selected African countries, the book contends that with proper training on conflict-sensitive reportage of social issues like elections, journalists can play very active roles in setting the agenda for societal peace. The book also presents an example of the impact PJ training had on the 2015 general election in Nigeria and how PJ training can be a catalyst for non-violent elections in Africa. Drawing from the 17-point action for PJ as put forward by Jake Lynch and Annabel McGoldrick, the book proposes a 17-point guide to reporting elections in Africa, with the hope that the points will serve as templates for journalists involved in political reporting on the continent and help to mitigate the spate of electoral-related violence on the continent, thereby fostering a culture of peace and entrenching democratic values.

What is Peace Journalism?

The term "Peace Journalism" was first coined by Johan Galtung in the 1970s. PJ has, however, been recently popularised by[3] Jake Lynch and Annabel McGoldrick who describe the model as the deliberate selection and reportage of stories in ways that create opportunities for society at large to consider and value non-violent responses to conflict. PJ uses the insights of conflict analysis and transformation to update the concepts of balance, fairness, and accuracy in reporting. It also provides a new route map, which traces the connections between journalists, their sources, the stories they cover, and the consequences of their journalism. The model also builds an awareness of non-violence and creativity into the practical job of everyday editing and reporting.

One main feature of PJ is its ability to frame stories in ways that provide society with enough information with which to respond non-violently to conflict or situations capable of degenerating into conflicts. One major misconception about PJ is that it is only relevant or important in countries enmeshed in conflict or those that are conflict-prone. That is not the case, for although PJ can play very active roles in mitigating conflicts, it is also very relevant in countries where there is no open violence. By providing varied viewpoints that will help a large section of the citizenry make informed decisions about issues bothering them, PJ can help stem the possibility of open violence before it even occurs.[4]

PJ was conceptualised out of the need to correct the negative consequences associated with traditional (standard) journalism. Traditional journalism practices, rather than encourage peace, are more likely to foster violent conflict because they often do not present society with alternatives that encourage peace. This follows from the fact that news media have typically been used to promote wars and conflicts. For example, the news media was accused of helping the allies further their goals in World War I and to overtly manipulate the German masses into believing that Jews were of a lesser race.[5] The German Nazi employed all kinds of tactics and bought varying weapons prior to and during World War II. However, none can be compared to the overt propaganda employed by Nazi Germany. Propaganda was a major tool in the hands of Hitler and his allies, to maintain the loyalty of Germans. Similar to the horrific genocide perpetrated by Hitler is the significant role played by the media in the ethnic conflicts that engulfed Rwanda and former Yugoslavia. Journalists played crucial roles in the promotion of violence in the two countries.

It is vital to note that the media's roles in society are not all negative. The media can also and has often played very important roles in positively shaping society.[6] For example, the media's persistent reporting about pariah states such as South Africa under Apartheid helped in its own way in facilitating political change. Persistent media messages and campaigns brought the issue to the front burner of global public discourse that made it unsustainable and in discordance with the global political milieu of that era. Such reportage formed world opinions, which, in turn, led to actions by concerned nations. Also, it can be argued that persistent global press reportage of the civil war in Bosnia and the growing evidence of genocide by Bosnian

Serbs undoubtedly pushed the Clinton administration and the North Atlantic Treaty Organisation (NATO) to intervene and impose military truce which ultimately led to peace in the troubled nation.[7] The media helped in shifting and expanding the sphere of conflict reportage beyond the immediate conflict environment to larger venues, thereby giving insight into possible causes, instigators, and solutions.

The PJ model is not without its critics. Even its name evokes contestations. For example, renowned media scholar, Ross Howard prefers the term "conflict-sensitive journalism" to PJ. He argues that the "peace" in PJ makes it a more complex model than PJ practitioners are presenting.[8] Steven Youngblood, author of *Peace Journalism Principles and Practices*, published by Routledge, maintains that the checklist for conflict-sensitive journalism in Howard's *Conflict-Sensitive Journalism Handbook* aligns almost exactly with those put forward by PJ scholars and practitioners.[9] Howard, like Lynch and McGoldrick, advises journalists to avoid victimising and emotional language, to avoid making an opinion into fact, to provide adequate balance for stories, and to report fairly about solutions and peace proposals regardless of the source. Clearly, Howard's conflict-sensitive journalism and PJ, as put forward by Galtung, Lynch, and McGoldrick, have more similarities than divergences. All through this book, I used the terms interchangeably. I am of the opinion that both concepts are the same, and that their names notwithstanding, both seek to promote a model of reportage that considers the impact media messages would have on society in general.

Another area of contestation among scholars[10] is where PJ puts the reporter. One of PJ fiercest critics, David Loyn describes the model as "at best meaningless, and at worst a uniquely unhelpful and misleading prescription for journalism in general, and broadcast journalism in particular." He further argues that the primary duty of a reporter is to be an observer and not a participant in a conflict situation. He contends that the reporter is not there to make peace but to address the complications of a messy world and construct a narrative, not to search for connotations. Similarly,[11] it has also been argued that the idea behind PJ is often based on individualistic and voluntaristic illusion which suggests that journalists only need to change their attitudes and behaviours in order to produce coverage that will embrace the tenets of PJ. Critics argue that proponents of PJ ignore the fact that there are many structural constraints such as inadequate personnel, availability of sources, and access to the scene and information in general which shape and limit the works of journalists. Therefore, they argue, it would be imprudent to suggest that the conduct of PJ is solely a matter of individual scope.

In stout defence of the model, Lynch and McGoldrick[12] maintain that PJ is often misunderstood as "advocating for peace." Rather, they aver, it is a journalism model concerned with giving peace a chance in national and international debates, by ensuring that non-violent responses to conflict get a fair "hearing." This position negates the argument that journalists should be detached from happenings in the society as it is inconceivable and insensitive for journalists to remain aloof and disconnected in the face of social injustice and tyranny. It is near-impossible, for instance, to report disasters like the Rwandan genocide, the war in the DRC, the ravaging scourge of HIV/AIDS etc. without a sense of attachment, distinct emotional slant, and empathy.[13] The position that PJ overemphasises voluntarism and individualism, ignoring the sustaining surroundings, organisational logic, and economic pressures that go with day-to-day journalistic duties, is also contestable considering that journalists work alongside a group of other peace-minded people or groups to ensure peace as they cannot possibly work alone or in a vacuum.

A major criticism of PJ is that it inhibits journalists from practising fair and objective reporting. Fairness and objectivity, critics argue, are the universally known and accepted tenets of the journalism profession. I agree, as would many journalists or journalism researchers, that without objectivity, journalism loses its respect. However, objectivity without sensitive reportage can also be the bane of journalism. The notion of "objectivity" is possibly one of the biggest obstacles to journalists playing a more responsible and beneficial role in public life.[14] Objectivity—which focuses on facts and overt events—devalues ideas and fragments experience, thereby making complex social phenomena more difficult to understand.

There are certain positive connotations associated with the term "objectivity," such as fairness and the pursuit of truth without favour. Although these are very laudable inferences, they are nonetheless relative, depending on the contexts and sociocultural, as well as a sociopolitical milieu. For example, Lee argues that objectivity is not a fixed "thing" but is relative, because whether or not objectivity is a desirable and achievable goal for reporting in a democratic society is a debatable question. While objectivity as a fundamental part of journalism should be entrenched, it is vital nonetheless to note that news said to be "objective" can, in fact, fuel violence if proper contextualisation and conflict sensitivity are not included. Lynch and McGoldrick identify ways in which news said to be objective fuel violence, they are as follows:

- News that overtly favour official sources over others;
- News that are obviously biased in favour of events over processes;
- News that favour dualism in the way conflicts are reported.

Bias in favour of official sources

By its nature, news is change centred, yet its understanding of how change is attained is often one-dimensional. Thus, news often favours realism and sometimes unwittingly ignores insights of peace and conflict studies which hold that conflicts can change in a number of ways, thereby negating the one-direction nature of news.[15] It is common to read the position of official sources such as the military, government officials, and even international organisations during conflicts. However, because of the quest for news objectivity, we often hear so little about other actors of peace compared to official sources. This is often a convenient approach by some "traditional journalists" because getting information from official sources is always less complicated than spending time and making the efforts to get information from other stakeholders involved in the conflict.

Bias in favour of events over process

According to McGoldrick, most journalists have ignored the rudimentary requirements of reportage which is providing the public with the what, when, where, why, and how of societal issues. The excuse normally put forward by journalists is that this will make the story too long and boring. McGoldrick, however, argues that violence is often left to appear by default as the only response that makes sense during conflicts because journalists do not take time to explore the underlying causes of such violence. Thus, it becomes imperative for journalists to provide the public with the underlying causes of violence because the understanding of the underlying issues is essential to effectively deal with a conflict. Lynch and McGoldrick argue that there are the economic dimensions to why journalists prefer to report events over processes.

Bias in favour of dualism

Hearing "both sides of the story" is often regarded as objectivity at its best and means the journalist is under obligation to ensure that sides in a conflict are given equal opportunities to present their arguments. As traditional and laudable as this may seem, it has its pitfalls, particularly as regards peace-building and enduring positive peace. Dualism, though a key part of objectivity, unwittingly frames the conflict as a tug of war in which each party's only aim is a victory over the other, ultimately creating a win-lose situation which is inimical to lasting peace. I believe that consistent media messages tilted towards a particular goal can, indeed, have an immense impact on the public.

The journalist is always at a crossroad whenever the opportunity to report an incident presents itself. He/she is either reporting the issue as a peace journalist or a violence journalist. Either way, the reportage often impacts society in one way or the other.[16] Steven Maras, in his 2013 ground-breaking book *Objectivity in Journalism*, argued that the concept of journalistic objectivity itself is biased because, despite the fact that it is linked to higher standards of professionalism, questions of morality and responsibility do not always get fully addressed or are (un)intentionally evaded.

The points put forward by Lynch and McGoldrick reverberate with those earlier held by Glassier as far back as the 1950s, who argued that objectivity in journalism effectively erodes the very foundation upon which responsible journalism rests.[17] Glassier put forward four ways in which objectivity is biased. First, he argues that objectivity is biased against the press' watchdog role. This role requires that the journalist goes beyond what is said to uncover what is unsaid or what is intended. Second, according to Glassier, objectivity is biased in favour of the status quo because of its reliance on official sources and establishment institutions. Third, Glassier contends that "journalistic objectivity" is biased against the journalists' ability to think independently. Fourth, he argues, objectivity is biased against the very idea of responsible reportage. Journalists now "hide" under the label of objectivity, thereby shifting responsibilities—by arguing that they are simply reporters and not creators of news, and therefore, the consequence of what they report is not their concern.

In Table 1.1, Lynch and McGoldrick present what they term the PJ model, which illustrates a comparison between peace and violence journalism. The aim of PJ, and indeed my aim in this book, is to inculcate more of the tenets of PJ on practising journalists and to discourage the practice of war/violence journalism.

As can be observed from Table 1.1, the focus areas of peace and war/violence journalism differ in their core motives. While the motive for PJ is to engender lasting peace (positive peace) where all parties feel that their position(s), interests, and needs are met in conflict situations, war/violence journalism focuses on the "winner" in a conflict and a cessation of hostilities (negative peace) rather than lasting peace.

War/violent oriented versus peace/conflict oriented

A classic example of traditional journalism is the 1990s American invasion of Iraq, which was a war fought on two battlefields—the media and Iraq, with the former accused of partly instigating the latter. Media

Table 1.1 Difference between PJ and WJ

Peace/conflict journalism	War/violence journalism
1. Peace/conflict oriented	1. War/violence oriented
• Explore conflict formation x parties, y goals, z issues, general win-win orientation • Open space, open time, causes, and outcomes anywhere also in history/culture • Making conflicts transparent • Giving voice to all parties, empathy, understanding • Humanisation of all sides, more so the worse the weapon • Proactive: prevention before any conflict occurs	• Focus on conflict arena—2 parties, 1 goal (win), war, general zero-sum orientation • Closed space, closed time, causes, and exits in arena who threw the first stone • Making wars opaque/secret • "Us-them" journalism, propaganda, voice, for "us." See them as the problem; focus on who prevails in war, dehumanisation of "them" more so worse the weapon • Reactive: waiting for violence before reporting • Focus only on visible effects of violence (killed, wounded, and material damage)
2. Truth oriented	2. Propaganda oriented
• Expose untruths on all sides/uncover all cover-ups	• Expose "their" untruths/help "our" cover-ups/lies
3. People oriented	3. Elite oriented
• Focus on suffering all over, on women, aged, children, giving voice to voiceless • Give name to all evil-doers • Focus on peacemakers	• Focus on "our" suffering, on able-bodied elite males, being their mouthpiece • Give name of evil-doers • Focus on elite peacemakers
4. Solution oriented	4. Victory oriented
• Peace = non-violence + creativity • Highlight peace initiatives also prevents more war • Focus on structure, culture, the peaceful society • Aftermath: resolution, reconstruction, reconciliation	• Peace = victory + ceasefire • Conceal peace initiatives, before victory is at hand, focus on treaty, institutions, and controlled society • Leaving another for war, the return of the old flares up again

Source: Adapted from Lynch and McGoldrick (2005: 6).
PJ: Peace Journalism; WJ: war journalism.

reportage in the build-up to the American-led invasion reduced the conflict to two parties, personified in the two presidents, George W. Bush and Saddam Hussein. The unfortunate framing of the conflict as the

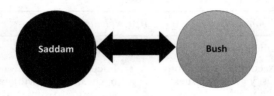

Figure 1.1 Line conflict between Bush and Saddam.

battle of two meant the conflict became a tussle; as such, both George Bush and Saddam Hussein struggled to gain a "metre" over one another. Media frame reduced the conflict to a situation whereby each party faced only two possibilities—victory or defeat. In the end, the world witnessed a war that would have probably been averted (Figure 1.1).

Lynch and McGoldrick explain that the component parts of war journalism are mutually reinforcing. The question is implicitly posed in the initial framing decision thus

- Like a simple geometric question, a line will be the only way two points can be joined.
- This means that this "line" will form the single axis upon which a change between them can take place.
- This leads to a tussle in which President Bush cannot gain a metre without President Saddam losing one.
- This leads to a zero-sum game in which each party in the conflict is left with only one option, to win or lose.

Such an approach to conflict framing does little or nothing to mitigate it because conflicting parties do not have options to propose a change in policy which does not move them to victory over the other. It creates a "win at all cost" stance that means anything that is not "winning" must be "losing." Thus, because of man's innate desire not to concede defeat, each has a ready-made incentive to step up or escalate his efforts for victory.

Truth versus propaganda oriented

Propaganda is defined as the wilful, intentional, and premeditated provision of materials calculated to further the interest of the propagandist. World War II was hinged on propaganda; the American-led invasion of Iraq was also aided by propaganda. The sad reality is that propaganda needs a conduit for its transference, and the media have severally presented itself as a willing channel.[18]

In the lead-up to the invasion of Iraq, the international media was awash with claims and counterclaims of the availability and possible use of destructive weapons or weapons of mass destruction (WMDs) by the government of Saddam Hussein. Proof that most of the media messages emanating at that time were skewed in favour of the invasion was obvious in the weakness of the claims put forward by proponents of the war. Lynch and McGoldrick state that Britain's Joint Intelligence Committee (JIC) and the government of then Prime Minister, Tony Blair, provided conflicting versions of the availability or non-availability of WMDs in Iraq. While the JIC described claims of the presence of WMDs as "sporadic and patchy," Blair described it as "extensive, detailed and authoritative." Whereas the JIC reported that there was a possibility that Iraq hid small quantities of weapons and agents, Blair's position was that the government of Saddam Hussein had large amounts of chemical and biological weapons capable of causing havoc to the entire Gulf region. The British Secret Intelligence Service warned the Prime Minister against overreliance on a single source for action against claims about Iraq's active weapons programme because the source's reliability was clearly unproven. Expectedly, work with the source was discontinued after the war when the source was discovered to be unreliable.

Years after the invasion and with new findings suggesting that there were no WMDs after all and that the real motive behind the invasion was oil and all its other sundry business, it became apparent that the media had once again failed the society. Lynch and McGoldrick contend that the media would have been less apologetic had they paid more attention to the inspection process and its findings. Sadly, rather than carry out extensive investigations into the claims and counterclaims regarding reasons adduced for the invasion, most international media organisations depended on *The New York Times*, which ingloriously ignored identifiable sources that might have cast doubt on the administration's Iraqi WMD claims while featuring unidentified sources that supported the claims.

Solution versus victory oriented

One of the major tenets of PJ is a shift from focusing on the problem of diagnosing and providing solutions to potential conflict situations. When we start with a tug of war in a conflict situation and dehumanise the other party, as was the case in the US-led invasion of Iraq, the remedy often is a military victory to get rid of that party. Conversely, when the problem is located in the conflict arena, it provides an opportunity to convince all concerned that a limited, pre-emptive, surgical strike can remove the "cancer."

Elite versus people oriented

The focus of war journalism often is on being the mouthpiece of able-bodied elite males, reporting their valour in war and esteeming the act of warfare in the process.[19] This focus led to an invasion of the war-front by American reporters to "experience the war" with the troops on the ground. While it is encouraging to show support for the gallantry of soldiers on the waterfront, it should, however, not be at the expense of dying children, women, and the aged, often neglected during war reportage. In contrast to war journalism, PJ seeks to shift focus from elite combatant to suffering all over, on women, aged, children, and giving voices to the voiceless. *The New York Times*, a leading channel for proponents of the invasion of Iraq, did little to highlight the suffering of defenceless Iraqis.[20] The newspaper's archive of stories reported during the war showed one human interest piece on Baghdadi teenage girls' difficulties in pursuing their education and going out alone.

Chapter summary

Despite decades of independence from colonisation by most African countries, democracy is yet to be ingrained as the norm in most nations in the continent. Most African leaders, it seems, would rather remain at the helm of affairs as demigods rather than conduct credible elections that would afford the populace the opportunity to decide who governs them and on what conditions. The relationship between democratisations, elections, and electoral violence is complex, to say the least. All over the world, the assumption is that regular free and fair elections are signposts to democracy; while this is true in some instance, it is, however, imprudent to assume that simply because a nation conducts an election, it now qualifies to be regarded as democratic.[21] Elections do not necessarily mean a nation is democratic; they only strengthen democracy and peace in the society. Elections not only allow for political competition, participation, and legitimacy but also permit peaceful change of power, thereby making it possible to assign accountability to those who govern.

Journalists and the media, in general, can help foster peace and the entrenchment of democracy in the society by applying their "power" to set agenda and frame news for the benefit of society. History is awash with journalists who have utilised the media's immense influence for the good of society.[22] Pauli recounts how separate interviews conducted with the then Egyptian President Anwar Sadat and Israeli Prime Minister Menachem Begin helped in no small measure to end the protracted conflict between both nations. The interviews, according to Pauli, focused on giving the two leaders the platform to air their grievances and to also understand the viewpoints of the other party. It helped in fast-tracking the peace process and in the historic visit of Sadat to Jerusalem.

Notes

1 Hyde, S. and Marinov, N. 2012. Which elections can be lost? *Political Analysis*, 20 (2): 191–210.
2 Omotola, S. 2008. Explaining electoral violence in Africa's "New" democracies. Paper presented at the *27th Annual Conference of the Nigerian Political Science Association (NPSA)*, held at Benue State University, Makurdi, Benue State, Nigeria, 16–19 November 2008.
3 Lynch, J. and McGoldrick, A. 2005. *Peace journalism*. Stroud: Hawthorn Press.
4 Hyde-Clarke, N. 2011. Political posturing and the need for peace journalism in South Africa: the case of Julius Malema. *Communication Online*, 37 (1): 41–55.
5 Stout, M. 2011. The effectiveness of Nazi propaganda during World War II (Online). Master's Theses and Doctoral Dissertations. Available: http://commons.emich.edu/theses
6 Ibid., 3.
7 Hackett, R. 2007. Journalism versus peace? Notes on a problematic relationship. *Global Media Journal-Mediterranean Edition*, 2 (1): 1–22.
8 Youngblood, S. 2017. *Peace journalism principles and practices*. New York: Routledge.
9 Howard, R. 2004. *Conflict sensitive journalism: a handbook*. Copenhagen: International Media Support.
10 Loyn, D. 2007. Good journalism or peace journalism? *Conflict and Communication Online*, 6 (2): 1–5. Available: www.park.edu/center-for-peace-journalism/documents/resources/good%20journ.
11 Hanitzsch, T. 2007. Situating peace journalism in journalism practice: a critical appraisal. *Conflict and Communication Online*, 6 (2): 1–9.
12 Lynch, J. and McGoldrick, A. 2005. *Peace journalism*. Stroud: Hawthorn Press.
13 Peleg, S. 2007. In defence of peace journalism: a rejoinder. *Communication Online* (online), 6 (2): 1–9. Available: www.park.edu/mobile/center-for-peace-journalism/documents/resouces
14 Lee, S. 2010. Peace journalism: principles and structural limitations in the news coverage of three conflicts. *Mass communication and society*, 13: 361–384.
15 McGoldrick, A. 2006. War journalism and objectivity. *Conflict and Communication Online*, 5 (2): 1–7. Available: www.cco.regener-online.de/2006_2/pdf/mcgoldrick.pdf

16 Maras, S. 2013. *Objectivity in journalism*. Cambridge: Polity Press.
17 Ibid., 15.
18 Jowett, G. and O'Donnell, V. 2012. *Propaganda and persuasion*. 5th ed. Thousand Oaks, CA: Sage Publications.
19 Ibid., 12.
20 Sengupta, S. 2004. "The Reach of War: The Occupation; For Iraqi Girls, Changing Land Narrows Lives." The *New York Times*, June 27, 2004. Available: http://select.nytimes.com/search/restricted/article?res=F10F1 6FB3C5C0C748EDDAF 0894DC404482
21 Omotola, S. 2008. Explaining electoral violence in Africa's "new" democracies. Paper presented at the *27th Annual Conference of the Nigerian Political Science Association (NPSA)*, held at Benue State University, Makurdi, Benue State, Nigeria, 16–19 November 2008.
22 Pauli, C. 2007. News media as mediators. Available: www.americanbar. org/content/dam/aba/migrated/dispute/essay

2 Political reportage of elections in Africa

The aim of this chapter is to analyse the media's election reportage in Africa, with a specific focus on Nigeria. The chapter will look at media coverage of elections across the world to determine the extent of similarity with coverage in Nigeria and possible lessons that can be learned. Case studies of media reportage of elections in Kenya and Nigeria will be reviewed.

The media as society's watchdog

The onerous task of safeguarding and ensuring the transparency of the democratic process lies on the "shoulders" of the media. While society "sleeps," the media, like a watchdog, is expected to keep awake by playing an active role in ensuring that the electoral process is transparent. Transparency before, during, and after elections is required at all levels, as the public must be able to access information without struggle, politicians should be held accountable, the legitimacy of individuals must be ensured and the public should be given the freedom to participate in debates without threats to their lives (ACE, 2013). Information in an electoral process is said to be transparent when the electorate is provided unrestricted access to information that will aid his/her decision-making. This access includes legal and operational procedures.

Transparency and accountability in elections are vital, particularly in Africa, considering that the entire electoral process in many countries is often vulnerable to fraud and manipulation, which often leads to widespread violence with loss of lives and destruction property.[1] To ensure electoral transparency, the election monitoring body (EMB), for example, is under obligation to inform the public of their actions, decisions, and plans. Because of the sensitive nature of the duties of the EMBs, only respected public figures that are known to be unbiased and working for the interest of the public are appointed to the board. Thus, before assuming such sensitive positions, their vital information such as affiliations, histories, and performance while in office is to be freely accessed by the public. The media plays a huge role in this regard, by highlighting the characteristics of members and would-be members of EMBs through features, editorials, and even straight news stories.

One of the media's chief responsibilities is ensuring that it acts as a catalyst for the avoidance of acts of violation and malpractice. The media also ensures that when such acts occur, they are investigated and brought to the public glare. To prevent acts capable of jeopardising the electoral process, the media ensures that it is present during the entire electoral process from actual voting to counting. They also ensure, through consistent reportage, that public office holders are held liable for their electoral promises and that political office holders live and operate above board while in office.

Norris identifies three political tasks for the news media system during the electoral process, and he opines that the media should act as a watchdog for civil and political liberties, to provide a platform for free and engaging political debate, and act as a mobiliser and sensitiser for public participation in a representative and participatory democracy.[2] An election is only deemed democratic when members of the public are fully able to participate and are unhindered in the exercise of their choice. To achieve this, the media is vital in ensuring that the platform upon which the electoral process is hinged is open and transparent. Politicians and members of the public must be able to debate and participate in discussions without fear of molestation and intimidation. Transparency of an election helps ensures that this indeed is so.

There is always a tendency by politicians to want to hijack the media, directly or indirectly. They are aware that the media can help them reach a larger audience in a shorter time; thus, they seek to manipulate or even outrightly buy media platforms and/or journalists.[3] Wolfsfeld posits that politicians share one thing in common—they want the news media to help them achieve their goal, which is often political power. Politicians realise that sympathetic coverage in some instances can bring in new members, help them raise money, raise their issues onto the public agenda, allow them to form public alliances, and put pressure on political leaders. Politicians also realise that although many times publicity does not bring a group anything more than a nice feeling that one's name is in the newspaper, it nonetheless is a huge asset for a politician's quest to gain access to the news media. The media should be wary and cautious of the fact that they may unwittingly become mouthpieces for politicians, rather than society's conscience.

In the run-off to elections all across the globe, competition for media space and coverage is often very intense. According to Wolfsfeld, it is a difficult competition especially for those without any political standing and for those without the financial wherewithal to compete in the ever-increasing campaign media budget. While money, lots of it, plays an important role in the political process, both for the EMBs and aspirants, the media can help in assuaging the burdensome political actors encounter, by providing fair and proportionate coverage of their political activities, irrespective of their financial standings.

During elections, voters rely on information provided by the news media on the electoral process. Often, voters have little motivation or ability to gather information about intricate social issues. Americans, for example, have been found to be extremely dependent on the newspapers and television news as their principal source of news and information on public policy and politics.

One major reason for possible overreliance on the news media for information during elections is the fact that information obtained from the media is "cheap" and easily accessible. This means individual voters would not need to go through the trouble of finding out information such as the policy of a particular candidate or party, their antecedents, strengths, and weaknesses. The problem is that this overdependence gives the media the excessive power to influence political outcomes through its agenda-setting and framing ability. Journalists should go beyond becoming the mouthpiece of politicians who use the media to report political speeches, campaign rallies, and photographs; instead, they should deliberately provide unbiased editorial commentaries, interpretative evaluations, and features that will help readers place issues in their proper contexts.

Through critical coverage, the media can effectively promote accountability and an electoral process that is genuine and free of interference by investigating claims about government's records and/or performance, candidates' qualification for office, and party activities and bringing such claims to the public domain. The media can also aid society by analysing party strategies and tactics and how they affect members of the public. The watchdog role of the media means that the media has the responsibility of providing background information about political aspirants and their parties. This is vital for the protection of civil liberties and political rights because it opens up the actions of government and politicians to public scrutiny.

Journalists' watchdog role requires that they are knowledgeable about the issues they cover so that they can provide society with informed contextualisation and backgrounding of issues. For example, Youngblood argues that since responsibly reporting about conflict is central to Peace Journalism, it is important for peace journalists to understand conflict theory and journalism's role in framing and mediating conflicts.[4] According to Youngblood, in conflicts, peace journalists can serve as third-party mediators between conflict participants. In the same vein, journalists covering and/or reporting elections should make concrete and intentional efforts to understand the electoral process, especially factors such as what motivates people to vote and why people resort to violence during elections.

What influences the way people vote?

Elections provide a people with the freedom to exercise their right to choose, either to install a candidate they deem worthy of a political position or to remove an existing office holder they reckon to be unworthy. It is (or should be) a participatory and representative process in which all citizens can vote and be voted for in a democratic setting.[5] Olanrinmoye describes participation as the level to which members of the public take part or are involved in societal activities that impact their lives. He refers to representation as the process whereby members of the public chose individuals to act in the interest of the community or sectors thereof. He concludes that political parties serve as the principal mechanism for ensuring citizen participation and representation in public policy decision-making particularly in countries where the dominant form of democracy is indirect or representative.

Elections confer legitimacy on leaders, and it makes them acceptable to the people; they confer a sense of citizenship on a people because the core of modern democracies is its citizens and elected representatives.[6] Schmitter and Karl observe that elections provide the citizenry with the power to ensure that rulers are held accountable for their actions or inactions. In exploring further the discourse on elections, it is vital to ask what motivates electorates to vote. Why do individuals vote certain candidates over others? What are the implications of voters' decision and the outcome of elections on societal peace? Understanding electorate behaviour is important to peace journalists because it provides information to use in reporting in ways that encourage interventionist peace-building activities before, during, and after elections to counter any drift towards violence.

In 1940, Paul Lazarsfeld and a team of social scientists at Columbia University applied survey research to the study of electoral behaviour. The sophisticated nature of the research means that the study is still relevant today when discussing elections and voters' behaviour. Lazarsfeld and his colleagues surveyed 600 prospective voters in Ohio as many as seven times during the 1940 presidential campaign; they made sure that the mixed new questions and repeated others in each successive interview and also had additional fresh cross sections to serve as baselines for assessing the effects of repeated interviewing on respondents in the panel.[7] This was done to determine the impact media messages had on their choice of presidential candidates.

Lazarsfeld and his team had hoped to demonstrate that carefully selected media content had a great tendency to sway voters' allegiance during elections. They, however, found out that media content had little or no impact on voters' choice of presidential candidates. Instead, voters chose candidates based on their perception of the candidate's "brand appeal." This brand loyalty seemed to be rooted in religion and social class which was reinforced via face-to-face interactions with people of like minds. The result shows that often, voters hold deep-rooted pre-existing political dispositions and are hardly "converted" no matter the persistence of the media messages. In a follow-up study in 1948, Lazarsfeld and his colleagues took another route by deliberately focusing on the influence interpersonal relationships had on voters' choice of presidential candidates; this they did by measuring respondents' perception of the political views of their families, friends, and co-workers. This meant that the team had to downplay the role of political parties and the mass media. They believed that by focusing on interpersonal relationships, they could ascertain the impact homogeneous social networks have on political campaigns.

From the result obtained from the study, Lazarsfeld and his team concluded that

> ... the usual analogy between the voting "decision" and the more or less carefully calculated decisions of consumers or businessmen or courts ... may be quite incorrect. For many voters, political preferences may better be considered analogous to cultural tastes—in music, literature, recreational activities, dress, ethics, speech, social behaviour. ... Both have their origin in ethnic, sectional, class, and family traditions. Both exhibit stability and resistance to change for individuals but flexibility and adjustment over generations for the society as a whole. Both seem to be matters of sentiment and disposition rather than "reasoned preferences." While

both are responsive to changed conditions and unusual stimuli, they are relatively invulnerable to direct argumentation and vulnerable to indirect social influences. Both are characterized more by faith than by conviction and by wishful expectation rather than a careful prediction of consequences.[8]

Berry and Howell put forward an alternative theory—that of retrospective voting. They are of the opinion that in retrospective voting, a voter can decide to vote an incumbent into office based on his or her previous performance in government.[9] According to Franks, however, often voters vote for the incumbent because it saves them the trouble of seeking information on other candidates. If the incumbent is already known and his performance is in the public domain for all to see, then it is assumed that the past performance of the incumbent can serve as a predictor of future performance.

Gélineau puts forward the economic voting pattern, where citizens would vote for a government when they are satisfied with its handling of the economy as reflected in the cost of food and availability of goods and services, support for the incumbent usually would drop.[10] It is, however, significant to state that a citizen decides on economic voting or economic accountability after reaching certain conditions.[11] Singer is of the opinion that citizens take time to first observe the economy to determine whether or not it is growing, and then based on the observation, the citizen is able to form an opinion (negative, neutral, or positive). The voter is also then able to decide whether or not his observations are a result of government management or mismanagement. In such a context, the model of electoral accountability would be conditional on the voters' individual attributes as well as features of the institutional context around them. Such a possibility clearly opens the way to observing variations in the extent to which voters blame/reward incumbents for perceived economic performance. As a result, one should find variation in the magnitude of economic voting across countries and over time within countries.

A classic example of economic voting and its impact on voter decision was demonstrated during the 1992 presidential election in the United States.[12] Roger and Tyszler argued that during the election campaign, Clinton's campaign team hinged their campaign on claims that incumbent President George H. W. Bush did not handle the economy well and was not deserving of another term. Thus, James Carville, a leading campaign strategist for Clinton used a whiteboard in the campaign headquarters to remind staff of the central message of the campaign.

The list read:

1   More of the same versus change;
2   The economy, stupid;
3   Do not forget health care.

Carville cashed on the fact that in every election, the economy is a central theme of discourse. Realising that the American public, like public across the world, judge candidates' performance on their ability to turn around the economy, Clinton's campaign team used catchphrases that inspired bumper stickers, political cartoons, and commentary throughout the period of the campaign.

Foucault, Nadeau, and Lewis-Beck have proposed patrimonial voting, which goes back to an old political economy idea linking an individual's vote choice with possession (or not) of the means of economic production.[13] This echoes Marx's division of society into workers and owners of businesses or means of production according to the assets they own: Assets, in this case, would be the apparatus of production in the case of the owner or the labour of their bodies in the case of the workers. Voting behaviour is ultimately determined by the number of assets possessed by individuals. They are of the opinion that wealthier are more likely to tilt towards right-wing parties known for their traditional unwillingness to support redistribution and support for business interest, while individuals with few or no economic assets besides their labour gravitate towards leftist parties that favour economic redistribution.

However, Stubager et al. are of the view that patrimonial voting theory goes beyond simply looking at assets, stating that assets are usually classed by individuals as either low risk or high risk.[14] Citizens choose assets according to their degree of risk aversion, with risk-averse citizens preferring assets such as houses, a savings account, and summer house that does not entail risky decisions and is not subject to large market unpredictability. Such assets require little ongoing attention and are characterised by (relatively) stable price development. On the other hand, individuals with a larger appetite for risk will be more attracted to assets that hold out the potential for larger profits like shares, a business, or rental properties.

A classic example of patrimonial voting behaviour played out during the 2007 French General Elections whereas proposal for a generous fiscal measure for first-time homeowners was put forward by Nicolas Sarkozy. Sarkozy's action was influenced by the fact that the French on average spends 35% of their disposal earnings on housing.

His proposition was part of the 2007 French fiscal package consisting of policies aimed at lightening the fiscal burden on businesses, liberalising the labour market, and stimulating investment. Sarkozy's tactics were patrimonial in that it made the French public believe that their material situation could be improved if he gets elected into office.

Journalists need to be aware of the factors that influence voters' choices because of the need to present detailed contexts and background to the political milieu and actors. Most countries in Africa have a multi-ethnic and very diverse population that react differently to media messages. Often, media messages are interpreted within the ambit of sociocultural and socio-political cleavages.

The media and election reportage: case studies

As one of several actors in the political landscape during elections, the media nonetheless plays a very key role in determining the success or otherwise of elections. Often, elections are cast like movies with the media playing the lead role or acting as a bit-part actor simply adding small elements to a plot constructed elsewhere. Like cheerleaders, the media also amplifies and echoes what has happened somewhere else. Whatever role the media plays in the "movie," the fact remains that the media is a vital factor in the interpretation of the electoral "script." Its interpretation can play a significant role in the peace, progress, and prosperity of the society at large.[15]

Citizens are motivated to exercise an informed choice during elections when they are assured that elections are free and fair, that they occur at regular intervals, and that their votes translate into seats and alternation of the authorities in government. Citizens are further motivated when they know that they possess the power to hold parties and representatives answerable for their actions and when the need arises, vote them out of positions. A credible electoral process goes beyond the freedom to cast votes and ensure that the votes count; it is also about a process of participation where voters engage in debates about political parties, candidates, their policies, and the election process itself. This helps them make informed choices regarding who to vote and why. The essential role of the media in elections cannot be overemphasised.

Political reporting of elections in Kenya

Kenya has a very vibrant and enthusiastic media. Like most African countries, the modern media in Kenya was started by British missionaries.

The early examples include the *Taveta Chronicle* which was published by Rev. Robert Stegal of the Church Missionary Society in 1895. The paper was the flagship for the European settlers in Kenya and gave rise to other newspapers in Kenya and East African region. The British East African Company founded the *Leader* in 1899, while the *Ugandan Mail* was published in Mombasa. The basic objective of these papers was to provide information for the missionaries and settlers of news that came from home. Such newspapers became a device to maintain the status quo by legitimising the rights of the colonial masters to rule Kenya. They also provided a channel for social communication among the settlers in Kenya from different parts of the country.[16]

The mainstream media in Kenya operates in English and Swahili as national and official languages. According to the Kenya Media Landscape Guide (2010), television reaches 40% of the population, while newspaper circulates among 30%. Kenya's mainstream media has gained a reputation for exposing corruption, promoting human rights, and providing a forum for public debates. The years of single-party politics limited the watchdog role of the media. The amendment of the constitution in the early 1990s to reintroduce multiparty electoral democracy brought challenges for the mainstream and proliferating alternative media to remain professional by following ethical standards such as objectivity, fairness, and impartiality. The media in Kenya have been unfortunately touted as biased and prejudiced in their reportage of elections. While the media is seen as the most trusted public institution, it has also been blamed for fuelling the conflict that ensued shortly after the disputed 2007 presidential election. The media was accused of political bias, fanning the embers of ethnic hatred and marginalising voices of reason in an ethnically polarised political environment.

The 2013 election provided an opportunity for alternative election reportage.[17] Warah argues that the local media in Kenya displayed extreme caution and restraint, bordering on self-censorship, in terms of how it reported the election. Acts of violence and disturbances in some parts of the country during the election were downplayed, perhaps in the belief that reporting these events might trigger reprisal incidents elsewhere or make the violence appear more widespread than it really was. According to Warah, the Kenyan media had decided not to "disturb the peace," even if it meant under-reporting electoral misconduct. In some regards, one may argue that the Kenyan press practised Peace Journalism during the 2013 election, though critics will contend that the media's under-reportage of issues during the election negates the principles of objectivity and fairness. This "peace messaging," according to Warah, was also premised on the awareness that a politically unstable Kenya was not good for local businesses and foreign investors and that remaining peaceful or non-violent was good for the economy. In the long run, the election was largely free of violence.

Suffice to add that the Kenyan election was not without its criticisms. Critics believe the media, in an attempt to avoid a possible repeat of the electoral violence that rocked the country in 2007 practice a journalism of "compromise." The general elections gave Kenyans an unsatisfactory choice between the half-truths of the foreign press and the illusions of their own national media.

By African standards, many pundits believe the Kenyan election was relatively peaceful, and the media has been credited with practising responsible peace-oriented journalism. However, even those who publicly praised the Kenyan media's overtures to unity will privately confess that they harboured concerns, particularly about the self-censorship drive adopted by the national media. In the fear of telling dangerous half-truths, an extreme relativism that all truths are equal was permitted.

Beckett believes that the Kenyan media presented an "illusion" of unity among the populace. It covered the glaring differences that still existed among the people and under-reported accusations of rigging and electoral malpractices levelled against Uhuru Kenyatta.[18] Although the fact that the Kenyan media made a conscious effort at preserving the peace of the nation before, during, and after the election is commendable, sweeping the nation's obvious differences under the rug was akin to postponing doomsday. In the not too long future, issues such as ethnicity, religion, and gross electoral malpractices that went unreported or under-reported could spring up with dire consequences. Beckett argues that although telling the "good" stories played a critical role in preventing violence during the electoral process, it is important to the real challenge of forming a national narrative, however, is how to include conflict, injustice, suffering, and inequality—how to promote mutual understanding on the themes that divide us.

The Nigerian media and political reporting

The Nigerian media is arguably one of the most vocal on the African continent. With a population of over 185 million people, and with over 500 ethnic groups and diverse religions, Nigeria's multicultural and multi-religious setting means that media messages are often given several interpretations beyond their original intentions. These (mis)interpretations have the potentials of eliciting violence and also to engender peace. As Akinfeleye holds, the Nigerian media is a two-edged sword, capable of motivating for peace or instigating for violence.[19] The relevance of the media in any polity is generally drawn from the fact that information is necessary for effective governance and administration, and the society depends profoundly on the press for vital information.

Over the past several decades, Nigeria's media has passed through various stages from state domination of print and broadcast media to liberalised format, involving state and the private sector. In assessing the role of the media in society, the media plays a multiplicity of roles such as fostering communication, aiding social cohesion, and building cultural continuity in a given society. At the individual level, the media fulfils audience needs for surveillance, personal guidance, personal relationships, identity formation, and diversion, among others. Rooted in the functional view of media, the uses and gratifications approach to media use assumes that audiences are aware of their social and psychological needs and actively seek the media to fulfil them. That is, needs fulfilment motivates audience media use.[20]

From Townsend to new media

Historically, the development of the Nigerian press is traceable to an Anglican missionary Henry Townsend, who in 1859 commenced newspaper publishing with the first newspaper in Nigeria, called "*Iwe-Iroyin fun awon Egba ati Yoruba*," which literally means "*A Newspaper for the Egba and Yoruba Nations.*" First published in 1859, the paper's aim was to encourage literacy and build up elites among the then Egbas of Abeokuta, present-day Ogun State in Nigeria's south-west. The newspaper was published fortnightly and became extremely popular among the elite in Egbaland, and it was a mainly Yoruba language newspaper. After growing patronage and widespread acceptance, the newspaper later started publishing in Yoruba together with an English translation.[21] Abati is of the opinion that the demise of "*Iwe-Iroyin*" later resulted in the emergence of other newspapers such as *Anglo-African, Lagos Time and Gold Coast Advertiser, Lagos Observer, The Eagle and Lagos Critic, The Mirror, The Nigerian Chronicle, The Lagos Standard, Lagos Weekly Record, African Messenger, The West African Pilot,* and *Nigerian Tribune.*

The growth of the early Nigerian newspapers gave rise to the nationalistic struggles that eventually led to the independence of Nigeria from Britain. Most of the publishers of the emerging newspapers at that time formed the nucleus of the nationalists that agitated for the independence of Nigeria. Prominent nationalists such as Herbert Macaulay, Dr. Nnamdi Azikiwe, Chief Obafemi Awolowo, Dutse Mohammed Ali, Ernest Ikoli, and Anthony Enahoro all used their newspapers as platforms for mobilising the citizenry against British rule. It can be argued that the pressure from the press contributed in no small measure towards the attainment of independence in 1960.

Oso observes that although the *Iwe-Iroyin* set the stage for what turned out to be a media-led campaign for Nigeria's independence, the turning point actually came about with the amalgamation of Nigeria's Northern and Southern Protectorates in 1914.[22] The amalgamation meant that newspapers based in the former Northern and Southern Protectorates "joined forces" to clamour for a common goal, Nigeria's independence. The amalgamation led to an increase in nationalist tempo, resulting in an increase in the number and variety of newspapers in the country. He states that while 16 papers were published between 1880 and 1914, 64 were published between 1914 and 1945.

It is important to note that aside from the amalgamation, the newspaper industry was stimulated by the 1922 Clifford constitution which introduced the elective principle that provided the platform for Africans to take part in the electoral process. The Clifford Constitution provided a motivation for the early rise of nationalist movements and also the evolution of political parties in the country. It was during the period that the first Nigerian National Democratic Party (NNDP) which was led by Herbert Macaulay was formed. Also, the Nigerian Youth Movement and the National Council of Nigerian Citizens were formed.

Historical evolution of broadcasting in Nigeria

Radio broadcasting was introduced in Nigeria in 1932 by the then British Colonial authorities as part of the empire service of the British Broadcasting Corporation (BBC). The service, which was called Radio Diffusion System (RDS), used wired systems and loudspeakers with which it relayed overseas service of the BBC to Nigeria. The National Broadcasting Service (NBS) Act was enacted in 1956. By 1957, the RDS also underwent a name change and became the Nigerian Broadcasting Corporation (NBC) to provide a nationally representative domestic service and external service. Seizing the opportunity of the colonial constitutional review which gave federal and regional governments concurrent powers in the ownership of broadcasting stations, the government of the western region established television and radio stations in 1959.[23]

By 1959, the Premier of Nigeria's Western Region, Chief Obafemi Awolowo had established the Western Nigeria Television (WNTV), touted to be the first in Africa. According to Udimisor, the introduction and expansion of television in Nigeria were hinged on political and educational factors. This position was collaborated by Umeh who asserts that Awolowo sought to utilise the WNTV as a tool for furthering the educational quest of the Yoruba people and for building societal peace and harmony.[24]

Nigerian media reportage of elections

Nigeria plunged straight into political anarchy barely six years after independence from Britain, in part caused by the disputed general elections that took place during the first republic.[25] During Nigeria's inglorious first republic 1960–1966, there were a mixed-party and non-party media, government-owned and -controlled media, political-party newspapers, and the press of private concerns. The ownership of these was largely reflected in their coverage of national issues of paramount importance, such as the census, election campaigns, regional crises, and ethnic and group interests, among others. The leading political party newspapers were not only locked in combat but all the media provided remarkable examples of overzealous, irresponsible partisanship and recklessness.

The major debate between the north and the south in Nigeria has always been whether the media mostly based and owned in the south could be fair and objective in dealing with matters outside its region. Since this is a deeply held perception, it has always been difficult to suggest that the mix of experiences that make up the peoples of the south is itself so diverse that they cannot be narrowly streamlined as "southern." To be sure, the south is diverse; for instance, one south-western part is a mix of Christians, Moslems, and other religions, while another south-eastern region is largely Christian. A huge gulf of ethnic differences separates them all. There are, certainly, problems in coverage. Generally, newspapers tend to be purely reportorial in their attitude to coverage, sacrificing analysis, and in that process failing in a fundamental obligation to offer their readership the critical choices upon which they might make intelligent decisions. Newspapers often do not engage in a lot of analysis or interpretation. This gap, plus a penchant for the deification of personalities, opens the window for bias and misrepresentation. This is often linked to the interests and/or aspirations of the owners of such newspaper outfits.

Media reportage of elections during Nigeria's second republic was as atrocious as that which led to the civil war. Consistent public discussion, as set by the Nigerian press, formed the fulcrum of discussions during the transition programmes which culminated in the advent of Nigeria's second republic. Apart from the military leaders' acknowledgement of mass media responsibility for interpreting and informing the electorate of the issues, the 1979 Constitution also required special obligations from the press on Fundamental Objectives and Directive Principles of state policy. The period from 1979 to 1983, known as Nigeria's second republic, was characterised by an increase in the number of newspapers in circulation and by the brazen nature of their editorials and reportage on issues of political significance. This considerably led to a high level of political participation and interest in a democracy by the vast majority of the Nigerian populace.

According to Olayiwola, at the peak of the run-up to the 1979 presidential election in Nigeria, every political pressure group in the country established its own newspaper to serve as a flagship and a voice in the often "noisy" political landscape in Nigeria. Newspapers became sources of conflict before, during, and after elections. Commenting on the impact of ownership on newspaper reportage of elections in Nigeria, Daramola asserts that newspaper ownership in Nigeria is closely tied to ethnicity and by extension to ethnic considerations in political reporting.[26] Daramola recalls the role played by *The Record* (1891–1930) of Thomas Horatio Jackson, Lagos *Daily News* of Herbert Macaulay, and *Eko Akete* in 1923 during the campaign for the first election in Nigeria. The available newspapers took positions as pro-NNDP; anti-NNDP and a few were neutral. Omu affirms that during political campaigns, even when the election had been conducted, the newspapers were overtly partisan and were a divisive force in the country.[27]

Other factors that can explain press bias in Nigerian political communications are ethnicity and religion. Many Nigerian elected or traditional rulers are aware of the damage these factors could do and have often warned people to guard against the menace of ethnicity and religion. Writing on the 1979 elections, Bolaji observed that just as the voting trend in the elections took on a "strong ethnic colouration," much of the country's press reflected the same pigmentation in their reports and comments.[28] According to Oso, the political elite in Nigeria have often made news a scarce commodity reserved for the few because of the highly contested public space for its propaganda and publicity value. Those with ownership and access, therefore, set agenda and frame public issues. Hence, Oso argues that news is not in any way neutral but ideological. This position is in consonance with the comment of Bennett and Entman that failure to control the news is often equated with political failure.[29] So, while the press was weaned from the control of the state and political parties, it went into the open arms of commercial and corporate interests. It was more of a case of the exchange of state control for the control of capital.

Whether the ownership of the country's media is vested in the hands of private or government, the media are mere megaphones in the hands of those in control. Citing the *National Concord* owned by then late Chief MKO Abiola, a National Party of Nigeria (NPN) stalwart, the ruling party in Nigeria in 1979, the publisher overruled that some stories which authenticity could not be verified should be published in order to achieve some political gains. A case in point was the publication of a land scam against Chief Obafemi Awolowo, who was alleged to have bought the whole of a sizeable part of Lagos. A similar streak of partisanship was noticed in the media's coverage of a long-standing debate surrounding the quota system in Nigeria. Oso observed that the press tended to reflect the debate in the manner in which its owners affect them—the major point to note is the extent to which the media has been so much their master's voices, that they pass individual opinions and positions on the federal character debate as group positions and interest. Similarly, ownership played a vital part in the content of newspapers vis-à-vis the Shari'ah crises in Nigeria. A keen observer of the trend in reportage during the peak of the clamour for full implementation of Shari'ah in most part of northern Nigeria would conclude that it was a "tug-of-war" between Christian southern owners and Muslim northern owners. *The Guardian Newspaper* has a Christian as owner, and this significantly played out during the Shari'ah debacle.

Ado-Kurawa believes *The Guardian* was overtly condemning of the planned implementation of Shari'ah in most of Nigeria's northern states. The Ibru Centre, an international ecumenical centre designed to enhance inter and intrareligious affairs has often been chastised for being pro-Christian in its views and ideologies. During the peak of the Shari'ah agitation, the Ibru Centre pages of *The Guardian* provided a telling tale of how *The Guardian*, which is supposedly rational and objective, promoted Christian views to the detriment of Islam and in particular the Shari'ah rouse. It is obvious that the press in Nigeria and indeed most developing countries in the world are entangled in the political milieu they find themselves. Indeed, analysis of media coverage in past Nigerian elections has been negative. The Commonwealth Observer Group report on the 2007 elections that significant state ownership of the broadcast media negatively impacted and influenced the coverage in favour of incumbents' parties.

Fear of government banning, ownership, ethnic, and religious bias has been the bane of journalism practice in Nigeria, particularly as it concerns election reportage. The major challenge has been ensuring that every citizen has equal access to information before, during, and after elections. According to the Centre for Democracy and Governance (CDG, 1999: 3), vital to the health of any democracy is ensuring that every citizen has equal access to information that would aid their political decision-making process. This, according to the CDG is important for two reasons. First, access to information equips citizens with the needed knowledge that would aid their decision-making rather than acting out of ignorance or misrepresentation. Second, the information provides the citizenry with the means with which to question elected officials when they fall short of their promises to the electorate.

Chapter summary

Chapter 2 took an exhaustive look at the media's method of reporting elections and the impact it has on peace in the society. Although the main focus was to analyse media's election reportage in Nigeria, it was important to look at media coverage of elections across the world to determine the extent of similarity with coverage in Nigeria and possible lessons that can be learned. Case studies of media reportage of elections in Kenya were presented, and the current mode of Nigeria's media reportage of elections was reviewed.

Notes

1 Abuya, O. 2010. Can African states conduct free and fair presidential elections? *Northwestern Journal of International Human Rights*, 8 (2): 122–164.
2 Norris, P. 2000. *A virtuous circle: political communications in post-industrial societies*. New York: Cambridge University Press.
3 Wolfsfeld, G. 2011. *Making sense of media and politics: five principles in political communication*. New York: Routledge.
4 Youngblood, S. 2017. *Peace Journalism Principles and Practices*. New York: Routledge.
5 Olanrinmoye, O. 2008. Godfathers, political parties and electoral corruption in Nigeria. *African Journal of Political Science and International Relations*, 2 (4): 66–73.
6 Schmitter, P. and Karl, T. 1991. What democracy ... and is not. *Journal of Democracy*, 2 (3): 75–88.

7 Bartels, L. 2008. The study of electoral behaviour. In: J. E. Leighley, ed. *The Oxford handbook of American elections and political behaviour.* Princeton, NJ: Princeton University.

8 Ibid.

9 Berry, G. and Howell, W. 2007. Accountability and local elections: rethinking retrospective voting. *The Journal of Politics,* 69 (3): 844–858.

10 Gélineau, F. 2013. Electoral accountability in the developing world. *Journal of Electoral Studies,* 32 (3): 418–424.

11 Singer, M. 2011. Who says it's the economy? Cross-national and cross individual variation in the salience of economic performance. *Comparative Political Studies,* 44 (3): 284–312.

12 Rogers, T. and Tyszler, M. 2012. Information and economic voting. Paper presented at the *2011 Annual Meeting of the Midwest Political Science Association and at the IMEBE Conference,* Barcelona, 2011.

13 Foucault, M., Nadeau, R. and Lewis-Beck, M. 2013. Patrimonial voting: refining the measures. *Journal of Electoral Studies,* 32 (3): 557–562.

14 Stubager, R. Lewis-Beck, M. and Nadeau, R. 2013. Reaching for profit in the welfare state: patrimonial economic voting in Denmark. *Journal of Electoral Studies,* 32 (2): 438–444.

15 Nesbitt Larking, P. 2009. Reframing campaigning: communications, the media and elections in Canada. *Canadian Political Science Review,* 3(2): 5–22.

16 Polycarp, J. and Ocholi, O. 1993. Press freedom and the role of the media in Kenya. *Africa Media Review,* 7 (3): 19–33.

17 Warah, R. 2013. Did the Kenyan media do justice to the 2013 election coverage? Available: http://sahanjournal.com/kenyan-media-election-coverage/#. WrOMNvlubIU

18 Beckett, Charlie (2017) How we report elections: time for a new agenda for political journalism after the 2017 shock? *POLIS: journalism and society at the LSE* (10 Jun 2017). Blog.

19 Akinfeleye, R. 2003. Fourth estate of the realm or fourth estate of the wreck: imperative of social responsibility of the press. Being an Inaugural Lecture Delivered on Wednesday May 14, 2003, University of Lagos Main Auditorium.

20 Wei, R. 2008. Motivations for using the mobile phone for mass communications and entertainment. *Telematics and Informatics,* 25 (1): 36–46.

21 Abati, R. 1998. Democratic struggle, freedom of expression and the Press in Nigeria. Paper presented at the *Human Rights Second National Conference,* Kano, Nigeria, 6–7 August 1998.

22 Oso, L. 2012. Press and politics in Nigeria: on whose side? Being an Inaugural Lecture Delivered 2012 at the Lagos State University, Ojo, and Lagos.

23 Udimisor, W. 2013. Management of radio and television stations in Nigeria. *New Media and Mass Communication,* 10 (1): 2224–3275.

24 Umeh, C. 1989. The advent and growth of television broadcasting in Nigeria: its political and educational overtones. *Africa Media Review,* 3 (2): 54–66.

25 Olayiwola, R. 1991. Political communications: press and politics in Nigeria's second republic. *Africa Media Review,* 5 (2): 31–45.

26 Daramola, I. 2013. Ethnic consideration in political coverage by Nigerian media. *Arabian Journal of Business and Management Review*, 2 (12): 38–52.
27 Omu, F. 1978. *Nigerian press and politics 1880–1937*. London: Longman Publishers.
28 Bolaji, S. 1980. *Shagari: president by mathematics*. Ibadan: Automatic Printing Press.
29 Bennett, L. and Entman, R. 2001. *Mediated politics: communication in the future of democracy*. Cambridge: Cambridge University Press.

3 Instigators or mediators

Exploring the role of the media in electoral violence

Introduction

With the spread of "democracy" across the globe, elections have also spread to nearly every continent. Before the turn of the century, the challenge before proponents of democracy was for dictators and authoritarian leaders to organise elections that would present the populace with options of those to lead them. It was generally (still is the belief) that with democracy comes improved social inclusion and general improvement in social security and well-being. Alas, elections have significantly increased, but the same cannot be said of representative democracy. As Cheeseman and Klass observe, dictators now conduct more elections but with advanced plans and strategies to ensure that they are not only rigged but they appear free and fair in the eyes of international observers and the international community in general.[1] What this has birth is an upsurge in post-election protests and complaints about the use of violence as an electoral tool, especially by dictators. One way through which dictators foster electoral irregularities is through deliberate hijacking or "buying" of the media. This chapter will delve into the role of the media in electoral violence. The aim is to ascertain the extent to which electoral violence can be attributed to media reportage.

The media, its agenda, and the rest of us

The theory of agenda-setting, though not a peace theory, is helpful in explaining how the media can foster societal peace through the prominence it accords issues of social importance.[2] Shaw and McCombs are associated with the theory, which describes the media's ability to highlight, through reportage or coverage, certain aspects of society in a way that influences the scope of public thinking. The theory holds that if the media focuses on an issue consistently, that issue(s) will become the dominant theme of discourse in the public sphere. In other words, the public waits for its "daily agenda" from the media. This dependence on the media by the society puts enormous responsibilities on the shoulders of journalists and the journalism profession because whether or not a society is in peace will depend largely on responsible agenda-setting by media.

A classic example of the media's immense influence on societal peace is the impact skewed, biased, and prejudiced reportage had in instigating and encouraging the 1994 genocide in Rwanda. It is imperative to note, from an African perspective, that although the agenda-setting theory is linked to Lipmann (1922), long before the advent of print and electronic media, Africans had traditional agenda-setters who set "agendas" which formed the bedrock of their daily discourse(s) at the market or village squares. In precolonial Africa, villagers often waited daily for the village town crier, a kind of information officer for the king, who used his gong, vuvuzela (or any other instrument, depending on the community) as a prelude to announcing news from the palace or about happenings in and around the village. News such as impending marriages between families in the village, an outbreak of illnesses, cultural festivals, and threats of war from neighbouring villages became the "talk of the village" for days or even weeks. The town crier, an oblivious agenda-setter, often determined the prominence accorded a particular social issue by the intensity with which he beat his gong or by the frequency with which he repeated certain information. He was a respected member of the community and an important member of the king's (or queen's) royal cycle.[3] The town criers combined all the information agencies in the performance of their duty.

Today, the town crier takes the form of journalists in newspapers, broadcast media, and most recently, social media, who set the agenda for public discourse. According to McQuail and Windahl, agenda-setting theory is predicated upon two basic assumptions[4]:

i   The media only filters what it perceives as reality; it does not reflect it.

ii   The concentration and focus on a few issues by the media unwittingly leads to beliefs by members of the public that the issues are considered more vital than others.

Given that different media have different agenda-setting roles, time becomes of the essence in agenda-setting. Thus, because of the complexity of the world, there is a need for society to depend on the media to decipher the world. Agenda-setting's uniqueness stems from its application in most leading communication journals. Agenda-setting theory best explained the media's role in society, particularly in the 21st century where more of society's directions are motivated by the media. Agenda-setting has provided a common umbrella for a number of research traditions and concepts in communication, a feature that possibly partially describes its ubiquity in communications research endeavours.

Setting agenda for war: revisiting the media's role in the Rwandan genocide

The media's agenda-setting role and its impact on society should be of interest to peace practitioners considering its potential to set the agenda for peace or for fuelling conflicts. Oftentimes, the agenda-setting role of the media has been reduced to their reportage of social issues but is important to note that the media can set agenda by also deciding not to report issues, by simply ignoring them, or by making such issues appear irrelevant in the eyes of the public. The following quote illustrates the Western media's agenda-setting with respect to the Rwandan genocide:

> Rwanda simply wasn't important enough. To British editors, it was a small country far away in a continent that rarely hit the headlines. The words Hutu and Tutsi sounded funny, hardly names that an ambitious news editor or desk officer would want to draw to the attention of a busy boss and claim that they were of immediate and vital importance. Within a few days of the plane crash, [which marked the start of the genocide] the Times ran several articles about what it obviously considered an angle to interest its readers: the fate of the Rwandan gorillas.[5]

It is ironic to note that at the peak of the Rwandan genocide, the Western media chose to focus on the fate of the Rwandan gorillas rather than on the thousands of human lives that were repeatedly lost daily. Although it is vital to protect a country's wildlife against possible extinction, it was nonetheless cold-blooded to place immense value (and media prominence) on gorillas in the forests of Rwanda over human life. After weeks of gruesome murders on the streets of Kigali and throughout Rwanda, the international media decided to shift focus to the cruel reality on the ground, a human tragedy of immense proportion.

The world's media reports about Rwanda were filled with images of ballooned bloated bodies, scattered along roadsides.[6] The fact that there were no media reports about the possibility of genocide in Rwanda while tension was still brewing meant that people got to know about the genocide only after hundreds of thousands had lost their lives. In retrospect, Thompson avers that had the international community reacted earlier enough, the needless deaths would have been prevented, rather than later showing pictures of disfigured corpses that made headlines across the globe after the evil had already been committed.[7] It can be argued that had the international media undertaken a more detailed comprehensive coverage of the Rwandan genocide, the killings of several thousands of lives would probably have been mitigated or completely halted.

I am of the opinion that had global media focused on the crisis at its infancy stage; they would have positively generated agenda for public discourse in the weeks, months, and even years that the conflict in Rwanda was brewing. Media focus would have had what Thompson calls the Heisenberg Effect on the Rwandan genocide.[8] The effect, coined in memory of Werner Heisenberg, a German physicist, describes the impact of observing a particle over time has on its velocity and direction. Although originally used to explain a scientific phenomenon, the Heisenberg Effect has profound applicability to the media. It is impossible for a scientist to continually observe any living organism without essentially changing it; observation alone changes the behaviour of the observed. The Heisenberg Effect means that no one does, or can, enact the same performance before an audience, compared to unobserved rehearsals. Furthermore, people need only imagine they are under observation, and this perception of being observed will inevitably alter behaviour. I cannot help but wonder what would have happened in Rwanda had the media consciously focused on and reported the happenings leading to the genocide. The world may well have been spared one of the most horrific genocides in human history. The media conspired with the government to perpetuate the genocide because the media reported media messages that were deliberately skewed in favour of government propaganda. It may be argued that the media out of fear refused to challenge the government's misrepresentation of the genocide as a tribal conflict.

The media also failed to deliberately question government information by seeking alternative news sources in pursuit of the truth. Rather than wait for the government to set an agenda for it, the media would need to have set its own agenda for public discourse in a way that would have prevented the conflict.[9] The behaviour of the media within Rwandan is further proof that journalists wield immense influence in shaping public opinion through deliberate and systematic agenda-setting. The hate messages churned out by *Radio Télévision Libre des Mille Collines* (RTLM) was, unfortunately, the only media agenda-setting that was taking place in Rwanda during the genocide, although with disastrous consequences.

Agenda-setting, agenda-building, and peace practice

While agenda-setting places enormous responsibilities on the media to chat society's path of discourse on social issues, agenda-building includes "some degree of reciprocity" between the media and government; the agendas of both influence public policy and subsequent action, for better or for worse.[10] The goal for Peace Journalism is to influence public policy for good. Although it is generally agreed that the media can direct public discourse by setting agenda, it is vital to note that the media is also part of society, and it gets its agenda from the society. The media's power to set agenda depends on the agenda the public feeds it. This understanding takes power away from the media and places it in the hands of the public. This "power" can help peace-building practitioners promote societal peace and harmony by generating positive agendas for the media.

Public agenda can be constructively shaped for positive and peace-engendering discourse if policymakers and journalists consciously generate discussions on peace-building. Rather than focusing public agenda on wars and rumours of wars that are capable of creating fear and promoting hate among the members of the public, the media can instead focus on successful peace-building initiatives and so set the agenda for positive discourse. This does not suggest that the media should cover up stories or withhold information. But it does suggest that the journalist should focus on non-violent responses in every conflict situation and help set public agenda in that direction. In other words, editors and reporters should conscientiously make choices of what stories to report and about how to report them that create opportunities for society at large to consider and value non-violent responses to conflict. In the words of the distinguished peace researcher John Paul Lederach,

I have not experienced any situation of conflict, no matter how protracted or severe, from Central America to the Philippines to the Horn of Africa, where there have not been people who had a vision for peace, emerging often from their own experience of pain. Far too often, however, these same people are overlooked and disempowered either because they do not represent "official" power, whether on the side of government or the various militias, or because they are written off as biased and too personally affected by the conflict.

(Adapted from Lynch and McGoldrick, 2005: 18)

In order to set a positive agenda for peace in the society, journalists need to be "attached" to the stories emanating from society in ways that suggest that whatever happens affects them directly or indirectly. Journalists cannot (should not) be detached observers of happenings in society. It is almost imprudent to suggest that a journalist can report rape, a tsunami, outbreak of epidemics, and so on, without some form of emotional "attachment." This attachment does not mean journalists should allow their judgement to be clouded; it only presupposes that journalists should endeavour to present the human side of every story. After all, it is humans who make stories, stories do not make people.

Critics often denounce journalism as a profession which imposes biased and distorted points of view, as compared with the shifting opinions and gazes which would otherwise freely circulate in public space.[11] For example, Muhlman describes this as connivance within the profession with those wielding power in the political and/or economic sphere thereby providing those in power with the means to impose their worldview on the public. Journalists run the risk of being considered biased or partial, hence the need to be fair and even-handed when setting an agenda for public discourse. Fairness may be difficult, if not impossible goals to achieve, but it is essential that journalists try. Journalists' even-handedness and objectivity is often put to test the most during elections and conflict situations. The media's capacity to influence public opinion makes it inevitable that they will promote some candidates rather than others. One consequence of such bias has plunged many societies like Nigeria into violence before, during, and after elections. As was observed in Kenya's last three general elections, the media (un)wittingly makes its agenda the public agenda by daily reporting a particular story and framing it in ways that give it prominence.

When set agendas become societal frames

Media framing theory can be said to be an extension of the agenda-setting theory; McCombs, Shaw, and Weaver refer media framing as the second level of agenda-setting.[12] The theory of media framing is based on the conjecture that audience's understanding of an issue is strongly dependent on the way that issue is characterised in news reports. In other words, the media can "frame" a social issue in such a way as to give it a meaning different from the original intent. Given that most media messages seek to elicit an emotional response from the audience, news stories are systematically framed and laced with emotional appeals. News framing plays on the fact that the audience responds differently to social issues based on the way they are presented by the news media. Frames from news activate certain inferences, ideas, judgement, and contrast concerning issues and policies. How news stories are placed, either presented with an imposing banner to get public attention and sympathy or tucked inside the newspaper for an interested reader to find, plays a great role in how audiences view the issues.

The basis of framing is that the media focuses attention on some events and places them within a field of meaning. They argue that journalists have the onerous task of deciding how a social issue is presented to the public.[13] Frames can be referred to as intellectual shortcuts that people use to help make sense of complex information. Media framing, then, is the use of these "shortcuts" to help individuals interpret the world around them and represent that world to others. Media frames are very important to peace-building in many respects because the media can frame conflict situations in ways that can significantly affect their intractability by creating mutually incompatible interpretations of events. Disputants in a conflict always construct media frames to suit their points of views because frames are often built upon underlying structures of beliefs, values, and experiences. In elections, opponents often use unsuspecting journalists (and sometimes conniving ones) to produce media frames that will serve not only as an aid to construing events in there favours but also to promote tactical advantages or benefits during elections. Politicians often use the media as tools for framing aimed at justifying acts of selfishness, convincing a larger audience, building political bridges of convenience, or adopting support for specific outcomes. Thus, one can safely conclude that the factors that influence the direction conflicts take are multifaceted. Like agenda-setting where the public can generate an agenda for the media through consistent discourse on burning social issues, society can also paint frames for the media in order to achieve set results. Politicians often use this method to coarse journalists into presenting often skewed reports about social issues.

When media personnel gather information, they consciously or unconsciously frame them to achieve a certain goal which could be personal, institutional, or even that of the media owner. Depending on how the media message is framed, the public unwittingly attaches meanings to them which, in a conflict situation, may affect their perception of the conflict. When the public or audience form perceptions of a given conflict, they gradually start forming positions which are usually for or against the parties in the conflict. This eventually leads them (the public) into taking actions that could either escalate or mitigate the conflict. A peace-motivated media message, on the other hand, can be framed in such a way as to result in the resolution of conflicts. By focusing on the core issues and by providing avenues for various opinions to be aired, an understanding of the viewpoint of others is achieved shifting focus from a win-lose state to a win-win situation.[14] Chong and Druckman argue that the media framing theory is premised on the fact that individuals and/or groups can view issues from different worldviews and perspectives and that these differing views form the basis from which decisions are reached.

Exploring electoral violence

In countries without a well-developed respect for the rights of their citizens, elections increase political polarisation and potentially increase human rights abuses. However, elections in liberal states ultimately bring about wider political involvement, civic commitment, and political accountability, all of which will improve respect for human rights over time. Electoral violence seems to be the norm rather than an occasional occurrence in most countries around the world, particularly in African countries.

Albert describes electoral violence as "all forms of organized acts or threats—physical, psychological, and structural—aimed at threatening, harming, and blackmailing a political stakeholder—before, during and after an election, with a view to determining, delaying, or otherwise influencing an electoral process."[15] Thus, one can safely adduce that electoral violence has effects that are multidimensional, having physical, psychological, and structural dimensions. As previously stated in this book, many factors contribute to the problem of electoral violence in Africa. In most African countries, electoral violence is perpetrated both by the incumbent in office who, against the will of the people, wants to hold on tenaciously to power and avoid defeat. Also, opposition elements seeking to wrestle power from the incumbent often also instigate electoral violence to the detriment of the society they claim to want to govern.

Suffice to add that electoral violence is not synonymous with Africa alone.[16] The 2004 national parliamentary elections in India were marred by unprecedented pre-election violence resulting from calls for a boycott by Kashmir separatists. In a bid to enforce their call for a boycott of the election, radical groups associated with the Kashmir nationalist effort staged a wave of assaults and bombings intended to scare voters. Similarly, scramble for ethnic Albania votes by supporters of two ethnic Albanian political parties led to the electoral violence experienced in the nation of Macedonia during the 2008 national parliamentary elections.[17] Although electoral violence in Africa is closely connected with the neo-patrimonial character of the African state, the nature of contestation for power, the weak institutionalisation of democratic architectures, including political parties and electoral management bodies (EMBs), this chapter delves on an often-neglected factor in most electoral violence in the world—the media.

Phases of electoral violence

Electoral violence can occur before, during, and after an election. Politicians initiate violence at different phases of the electoral process depending on their motives. For example, incumbents utilise pre-election violence to instil fear in opponents, thereby reducing their electoral competition. This ploy often induces opposition parties to boycott elections making it less likely that a promising opposition candidate will run. For example, the presidential candidate of the Movement for Democratic Change (MDC) Mr. Morgan Tsvangirai was forced to withdraw from the 2008 presidential election in Zimbabwe when his supporters claimed they were attacked by supporters of the ruling Zimbabwe African National Union–Patriotic Front (ZANU-PF).

Although violence often occurs before and after elections and in most cases not during the election proper, it is during campaigns or when results start trickling in that violence starts often become very overt and visible.[18] Election Day violence comprises of activities such as the forceful snatching of electoral ballot boxes, threats, and assaults on opposition agents and party members and even outright intimidation and harassment by security agents. Post-election violence as physical force intended to hurt or kill individuals or groups and arises in reaction to an announced election result. This logic, according to him, is different from pre-election violence, which can be used to influence turnout and vote choice on Election Day.[19] After elections, incumbents who remain in power, whether legitimately or not, may still be challenged by an election-induced threat. They are of the opinion that public protests, often resulting from dissatisfaction with the electoral process, frequently lead to post-election violence. Post-election protests indicate that citizens are willing to mobilize against the regime and have solved their collective action problem.

From the aforementioned phases of electoral violence, one would agree with Hoglund that motive and timing are the major factors that separate electoral violence from all other known forms of violence.[20] The timing of electoral violence is specific, before, during, and after elections, while the motive is simply to influence the outcome of the electoral process.

Why do elections turn violent?

As earlier stated, electoral violence has, as its central motive, the disruptions of the electoral process in such a way as to influence the final outcome of the process in favour of certain individuals or groups. Oftentimes, when incumbents feel that their popularity is waning and that they are probably on the verge of losing out during elections, they result in violence. Electoral violence constitutes a serious challenge to democracy in Africa in two major ways. First, the worth of democracy as the government of the people, for the people, and by the people is greatly undermined by electoral violence because the act or threats of violence often discourage voters and political aspirants from participating effectively in the democratic process. Second, electoral violence may also reduce public confidence in elections and sadly legitimize other forms of power transfer.[21]

Electoral violence in Africa differs from one country to the other in their nature, causes, and effects. On the one hand, in countries such as Nigeria, Kenya, and Ethiopia where there has been electoral violence in recent years, electoral violence is often a result of rippled effects of other underlying factors such as poverty, inter-communal competition, and perceived ethnic or regional domination. On the other hand, in countries such as Zimbabwe and Ivory Coast, issues such as complicated interfaces over land complaints, the constructions of nationhood and nationality, and the centralised use of political violence have been more important than ethnicity and regionalism.

Ethnicity and perceived marginalisation

Many trace the foundation of electoral violence in Nigeria to the amalgamation of the Northern and Southern Protectorates in 1914 by the

British colonialists, who without due consideration for the country's diverse ethnic groups, forged a "marriage" of convenience rather than compatibility. Issues of ethnicity and perceived marginalisation can be regarded as a colonial package bequeathed to Nigerians without their consent. The seed of ethnic division currently plaguing the African continent is traceable to the colonial state which, rather than recognize Africa's diversity, used the tools of modern state power to define and classify Africans through scientific instruments such as maps and censuses that assigned individuals and communities to what was believed, often incorrectly, to be ancient prehistoric identities.[22] Ethnicity is socially relevant when people's everyday life, decisions, and actions are conditioned and motivated by their ethnic affiliations or cleavages. Politically, it is when political alliances are pre-arranged along ethnic lines or when entrée to partisan or economic benefits depends on one's ethnic alliance(s).

Most of the civil wars that have been fought on the African continent have their root in divisions brought about by ethnicity. Ethnicity and ethnic alliances played prominent roles in the anti-colonial struggle. In Nigeria, for example, the likes of Dr. Nnamdi Azikiwe, Chief Obafemi Awolowo, Sir Tafawa Balewa, and Sir Ahmadu Bello fought for the independence first as ethnic leaders and then eventually as national leaders. It can be argued that although the "founding fathers" of Africa's independence are still credited for their sacrifices during the struggle for independence, they held on to their ethnic "lordship" for fear of losing regional significance. According to a Human Rights Watch report for 2011, politicians find comfort and relevance in their tribes, wielding the influence of tribal lords and rather than initiate the process of nation-building, they inadvertently sowed the seeds of discords all in a bid to protect their "tribe" from economic and cultural domination from their perceived rival ethnic groups.

The position of the Human Rights Watch is similar to that held by Eifert, Miguel, and Posner who state that traditional loyalties to kith and kin in Africa mean that ethnic identities are much stronger than national identities.[23] They argue that people first identify with their ethnic groups before they identify with the nation. While the position of Eifert, Miguel, and Posner is considerably true in most African countries, it is, however, important to state that issues of ethnicity and religious bigotry mostly rear their ugly heads during elections as politicians seek to win power at all cost. In the most part, people are more concerned about their daily livelihoods than of other people's ethnic alliances. For example, most of the elections in Nigeria have been decided by ethnic mergers and/or agreements. The deep-seated ethnicity in the country has led to the "election" of mediocre leaders who rode to leadership positions largely by the support of their kinsmen. Credibility and competence, it seems, have been sacrificed on the altar of ethnic affiliations and loyalties, leading to the denigration of adeptness to the background. This has also led to the recurrent cases of ethnic clashes in the country. Ethnicity has polarised the Nigerian political climate into extreme conservatives and progressives with each side seeking to have the upper hand by pursuing its interest albeit with severe consequences such as violence.

Huber views ethnicity, particularly as it concerns elections as either group- or party-centred measures.[24] According to Huber, ethnicisation and electoral violence increases when voting behaviour by members of a particular group becomes more unified, thus making the possibility of group-centred ethnic voting outcome predictable. Huber states that in the United States, for example, blacks have been found to vote overwhelmingly for democrats in the past, making it easy to predict the vote of a person simply by knowing his/her race. Belgium presents another telling example of the influence of ethnicisation in politics. Belgian voters also vote along ethnic lines, as the Flemish are more likely to vote Flemish candidates, while the French will also most likely vote French candidates. Thus, if one knows an individual's language, one knows which of the several parties he/she might support, and the parties the individual will most likely oppose. The implication of this type of voting culture, especially in countries with less developed democracies like those obtainable in Sub-Saharan Africa, is that it becomes easy for group mobilisation for conflict whenever election results do not reflect the expectation of a particular group. The knowledge of ethnicity's impact on voting behaviour and on the propensity for electoral violence can help the journalist decipher when aggrieved parties and/or ethnic groups are contesting an election result from an ethnic, rather than a systemic or ideological point of view. If the irregularity is due to inefficiencies from EMBs, journalists should report it as such. If protests arise as a result of group or ethnic grievances and not actual electoral manipulations, journalists should report it as such.

Poverty and inequality

Africa's teeming unemployed population have often been used as ready-made tools in the hands of politicians who exploit their apparent idleness to perpetrate electoral violence. While there are disagreements about the specific interface between poverty and conflict, there is no debating the fact that they both impact negatively on democratisation and development, and often lead to social instability. Hence, most of the electoral violence experienced in Africa is caused by poverty and societal inequality.

The intractable obstacles to free and fair elections since independence in Nigeria can be linked to poverty and unemployment. For a nation that has over 70% of its population in the youth bracket (2006 Census figures), the number of unemployed youths is enormous, and it has fuelled the existence of social vices such as kidnapping, smuggling, and terrorism. Politicians, sensing the obvious gap, have used the youths as political tools for the perpetration of violence.[25] Poverty is a common problem that plagues most African countries. The high rate of poverty among most Africans has made the continent a breeding ground for aggrieved youths who are susceptible to all forms of negative manipulations, especially during elections. Although most African countries now hold regular elections, they cannot in any way be regarded as free and fair. The processes are severely compromised and hugely contested, thereby creating legitimacy crisis for most governments in the country.

In a nation where the average citizen lives below a dollar a day, hunger and deprivation are commonplace. Thus, an individual deprived of the basic wherewithal cannot participate effectively in a democratic process and is a ready prey in the hands of politicians. However, Douma believes that it is imprudent to conclude that poverty directly results in political violence.[26] He avers that level of poverty in absolute terms cannot be directly related to the occurrence of violent conflict within societies. However, once group identity and poverty are linked, or a perception of discriminatory treatment can be discerned, the tendency towards violent opposition to the state or other groups becomes apparent. It is pertinent to note that persistent disparity leads to growing poverty and hopelessness, which strengthens the demand for political revolution. Poverty in itself does not cause conflict, but group inequality does, as it increases complaints. The highest risk of violent conflict occurs in societies like that obtainable in Sub-Saharan Africa where there is an overlap between poverty and ethno-religious cleavages.[27]

According to Fjelde and Østby, poverty as a source of violence, principally electoral violence, can be traceable to ethnic group demarcations and perceived inequality.[28] They observed that in Africa, ethnic group demarcations and sub-national regional borders often overlap, with each region fearing domination by a particular ethnic group. They are also of the opinion that there is a link between economically disadvantaged regions and groups that feel excluded from economic power. During elections, it is usually common to observe group resentments which often emanates from the perceived closeness of certain other groups to the central government.

Renowned Yale Professor, Amy Chua, in her book *Political Tribes*, argues that inequality, whether real or perceived, often breeds antagonism against perceived dominant groups. She contends thus,[29]

> Capitalism creates a small number of very wealthy people, while democracy potentially empowers a poor majority resentful of that wealth. In the wrong conditions, that tension can set in motion intensely destructive politics. All over the world, one circumstance, in particular, has invariably had this effect: the presence of a market-dominant minority—a minority group, perceived by the rest of the population as outsiders, who control vastly disproportionate amounts of a nation's wealth. Such minorities are common in the developing world. They can be ethnic groups, like the tiny Chinese minority in Indonesia, which controls roughly 70 percent of the nation's private economy even though it is between 2 percent and 4 percent of the population. Or they can be distinct in other ways, culturally or religiously, like the Sunni minority in Iraq that controlled the country's vast oil wealth under Saddam Hussein.[30]

Chua's position probably explains why there is a tenacious desire by ethnic groups on the continent to seek political power, especially to be at the "centre." It is generally believed that any group that is close to the government will enjoy certain economic benefits. This perceived imbalance can lead to collective violence with the aim of altering the election results, which, in turn, will alter the distribution of goods such as access to farming land but also to more obliquely haul out state benefaction through agitation. The intensity of the struggle is increased by the lack of regulating institutions that could prevent the "disadvantaged groups" from checking exploitative behaviour. Within the patrimonial state, there is no strong institutional framework of checks and balances that regulate the competition for political and economic assets between groups. This in itself enhances the attractiveness of taking radical action to alter economic and political relations, compared to seeking inter-group compromises when efficient enforcement is out of sight.

Politics of patronage

Often, where elections have turned violent, political leaders are, in most cases, key instigators. Political leadership serves two main functions in electoral violence that frequently plagues African states. First, political leaders encourage electoral violence through framing, that is, socially constructing certain identities for and images of supporters and rivals of the party that are often bipolar ("us" vs. "them"), for example, through militant rhetoric and hate speech. The second involves the mobilisation of perpetrators to carry out actual violence by creating concrete and selective incentives for those involved in carrying out the violence. Such inducements come in the form of benefaction, for example, cash payments, provisions of food, alcohol, and drugs, or in the form of longer-term enticements such as expectations of getting employment for family members and gaining powerful positions or state contracts for various jobs.

The role of the media in electoral violence

To what extent does media reportage instigate the several election-related violence that have plagued most African countries? The role the media played in the Rwandan genocide and the destructive use of the media as a propaganda weapon during Hitler's Nazi regime suggests that the media and its effect on society cannot and should not be underestimated. The media provides members of the society awareness into political dynamics and the level of dialogue within the society. The media also has the "power" to suggest the level of divergence in a society like it did with hate messages targeted at minority Tutsis in Rwanda; the progress of compromise; and, in the case of post-election violence, the possible avenues for the peaceful resolution of disputes. One of the main objectives of the media is to act as a source of information for the populace. The fast-paced nature of society today means that most people do not have the time to source for news themselves, so they depend on the media to provide them with information on the political happenings in the country, government policies, the electoral process, foreign policies, and international developments. The public relies significantly on the media to provide the needed information that will aid them in making informed choices.[31]

The media can inform society about issues that were hitherto not topics of public debate by consciously setting such issues as agenda for public discourse. Through its interpretative role, the media can also bring new interpretations, opinions, and arguments to an existing story in ways that may instigate violence or mitigate existing conflict. The media wields enormous influence regarding how the public views and interprets social issues. The media affects electoral violence in two key ways: first, they are sources from where members of the public gather evidence that in the election is illegitimate or being contested domestically whether or not it was fair or certified by the EMB. The media provides interpretative frames that can lead to the conclusion by the members of the public that the election has not been free and fair and that could lead to tension in the polity.[32]

Second, the media can also instigate violence by showing graphic pictures of the member so of the public who have been killed or hurt in the process of exercising their right to choose their leaders. This, unfortunately, has the ability to incite reprisal attacks from aggrieved groups thereby leading to more violence.

Case studies

• Kenya

Many were shocked by the 2007 post-election violence that rocked the nation of Kenya, once touted as one of Africa's most peaceful countries. The conflict that ensued after election results were announced was due in part to the ethnic and geographic diversity of politics in Kenya and to a large extent due to uncontrolled media reportage. According to Ojwang, the violence was precipitated by heightened expectations, hyped pre-election opinion polls, and media reports of alleged unavoidable rigging.[33] During the run-up to the 2007 general election, the Kenyan public depended on the media to play its role as society's watchdog by monitoring the election and reporting it in an unbiased manner. Through their live updates at the national vote tallying centre, the media set the tempo of public interest as a national conflict unfolded amid finger-pointing and showboating by political party loyalists.

Most conflicts in the world emerge through the creation of the "we" versus "them" scenario that often labels one party "the enemy" in issues of divergences. During the build-up to the 2007 general elections in Kenya, a consortium of private media owners, *the Standard Group*, *The Nation Media Group*, and *Royal Media Services*, in an attempt to mobilise the Kenyan populace, ran a campaign with the title "give us back our country." Although it was supposed to basically be a campaign of the public against the inaction of the state, using the inclusive phrases "us" and "our" somewhat pitched the public against the government. Soon afterward, headlines from leading Kenyan newspapers created a sense of hopelessness in the Kenyan people and gave the impression that the nation had reached a boiling point. A classic example was the recurring headline "Kenya Burns" that made the front page of the

Standard for the first two weeks of January 2008. In the same vein, *The Daily Nation's* edition of 3 February 2008 had as its headline "the Republic of Kenya was a smoldering burnt out shell" (*Daily Nation*, 3 February 2008: 1).

Radio broadcast shortly after the election contributed in no small measure in fuelling the post-election violence that rocked the country. The major culprits were the vernacular radio stations which broadcast in *Luo, Kikuyu, Kalenjin,* and other local languages. The stations overtly broadcast hate messages which had similarity with the messages that were deployed during the unfortunate Rwandan genocide. The mainstream English media seemed obliged to remain unbiased as its messages were largely fair, while the vernacular stations fuelled the embers of hatred and divisions.[34] Vernacular radio stations provided Kenyans with a ready-made platform with which to vent their anger against the government and against other ethnic groups. Live phone-in programmes that were difficult to censor, provided some Kenyans with the stage with which they encouraged divisions and called for ethnic war. Words which were akin to the hate speech perpetrated by Radio Television Libre des Mille Collines (RTLM) during the Rwandan genocide were freely used. RTLM had broadcast covert hate speeches placed alongside the sophisticated use of humour such as "you [Tutsis] are cockroaches! We will kill you!"

Like the Rwandan genocide, hate speech in the Kenyan media during the election consisted of open incitements and subtle use of metaphors and epithets that were understood only by speakers of the local language in which they were broadcasted. A report by Integrated Regional Information Networks (IRIN, 2008) claims that there were incidences where vernacular music understood only by the native speakers was used to incite ethnic tensions in the country. For example, *Kameme* and *Inooro*, two Kikuyu stations, were accused of playing songs that denigrated the person of the opposition leader Raila Odinga and his Orange Democratic Movement (ODM). The stations referred to them as "*beast from the west.*" Similarly, a Luo station, *Radio Lake Victoria*, played a song by D. O. Misani in which he referred to the government as the leadership of baboons. The impact of the post-election violence in Kenya was colossal. The death toll from the violence was estimated at around 1,300.

- Nigeria

The Nigerian media is arguably one of the most vocal on the African continent and yet one of the most polarised. With over

250 ethnic groups and close to 400 languages, Nigeria presents a telling case of how irresponsible and unguarded reportage can ignite conflict. The Nigerian media have the arduous responsibility of reporting social issues to the public within the limits of media laws and ethics. However, they have severally reneged on their responsibilities and have the notorious record of either telling half-truths or complete lies altogether. The Nigerian press was very active during the quest for political emancipation, by acting as recruiters and mobilisers of the public. The newspapers of that period were divided along party lines, and they served as vehicles for changing political consciousness and for the propagation of the ideals of nationalism. The press also largely recruited people to political movements, contributed to party organisation, and encouraged the penetration of political activities into the then existing provinces. During the electoral process of 1953, for example, Nigerian newspapers were identified as falling into three groups: the Igbo-led pro-Nigerian National Democratic Party (NNDP), which was exemplified by the *Record Newspaper*; anti-NNDP, embodied by *The Advocate* and *The Tribune* which was the campaign medium for the ethnic Yoruba-led Action Group; and the National Council of Nigeria and the Cameroons (NCNC), a predominantly northern party, had the *Pilot Newspaper*.[35]

This political division was evident during the electoral process of the first republic of 1960–1966. The newspapers were not only locked in the malicious scuffle for prominence, but they also provided remarkable examples of obsessive and irresponsible partisanship. The seeds of mutual distrust, running battles, and endless hostilities between regional media and the federal media, on the one hand, and between different regional media and political party newspapers, on the other hand, all of which were sown during the colonial, independence, and First Republic periods, meant that it was only a matter of time before the country spiralled into conflicts.[36] Sign that the nation was on the verge of a crisis was evident during the census of the First Republic, as it sparked bitter interethnic hostility and divided the political leadership along ethnic-regional front lines. The largely ethnic and regional media and its overtly prejudiced reportage played very significant roles in the controversy that marred the 1964 federal elections, the attendant constitutional stalemate and the eventual violent collapse of the First Republic.

The Second Republic was not different from the failed First Republic, as the media was also very sectional in their reportage as they openly lined up behind political parties and candidates, depending on their ethno-religious lineage, leading to ethnic divisions and tensions in the country. Given that the country was already polarised before the election, the press failed to bridge the obvious divisions in the country and instead fell prey to politicians' divisive whims and caprices. Thus, the media was sadly unable to develop the required ethos of professionalism, impartiality, responsibility, objectivity, and balance in its reportage of political events, particularly elections.

The veracity of the media and the credibility of their practitioners became questionable. This was one of the factors that contributed to the fall of the Second Republic in December 1983. The consequences of all these were disastrous for the nation. Nigeria again began to manifest the drift and hopelessness which preceded the collapse of the First Republic. The signs were obvious and ominous: intense and violent political rivalry, unguarded and inflammatory public statements, and deliberate destruction of public and private properties. Eventually, the military "intervened" again.

Chapter summary

Several factors contribute to the prevalence of electoral violence across the world; in Africa and most developing countries of the world, poverty and inequitable distribution of resources have been several linked to the susceptibility of the populace to be ready preys in the hands of desperate politicians. Although I agree with the position put forward by Douma who believes that it is imprudent to conclude that poverty directly results in political violence because, according to him, level of poverty in absolute terms cannot be directly related to the occurrence of violent conflict within societies.[37] I, however, contend that the fact that most of the electoral violence experienced in the world occur in Third World and developing countries where the prevalence of poverty is much higher than the "developed countries" suggests that poverty and perceived inequality can act as a trigger for electoral violence particularly when there is a financial exchange involved. Aside from poverty, other factors such as fear of the possibility of losing elections by the incumbent, faulty electoral systems, and ethnically polarised public sphere also impinge on electoral credibility and fuel electoral violence.

However, as can be observed from the case studies put forward, the media, when not appropriately applied, is also a major cause of electoral violence. In Kenya, Zimbabwe, and Nigeria, media reportage has been linked to the electoral violence that the countries have experienced. The media provides members of the society awareness into political dynamics and the level of dialogue within the society. The media also has the "power" to suggest the level of divergence in a society like it did with hate messages targeted at minority Tutsis in Rwanda; the progress of compromise; and, in the case of post-election violence, the possible avenues for the peaceful resolution of disputes.

Notes

1 Cheeseman, N. and Klass, B. 2018. *How to rig and election*. New Haven, CT: Yale University Press.
2 McCombs, M., Shaw, D. and Weaver, D. 1997. *Communication and democracy: exploring the intellectual frontiers in agenda-setting theory*. Mahwah, NJ: Erlbaum.
3 Aziken, L. and Emeni, F. 2010. Traditional systems of communication in Nigeria: a review for improvement. *Knowledge Review*, 21 (4): 23–29.
4 McQuail, D. and Windahl, S. 1993. *Communication models for the study of communications*. 2nd ed., London: Longman.
5 Dowden', R. 2007. The media's failure: a reflection on the Rwanda genocide'. In: A. Thompson, ed. *The media and the Rwanda genocide*. London: Pluto Press.
6 Thompson, A. 2007. *The media and the Rwandan genocide*. London: Pluto Press.
7 Ibid., 61.
8 Ibid., 55.
9 Schimel, N. 2011. An invisible genocide: how the Western media failed to report the 1994 Rwandan genocide of the Tutsi and why. *The International Journal of Human Rights*, 15 (7): 1125–1135.
10 Rogers, E., and Dearing, J. 1988. Agenda-setting research: where has it been, where is it going? *Communication Yearbook*, 11: 555–594.
11 Muhlman, G. 2010. *Journalism for democracy*. Cambridge: Polity Press.
12 Ibid., 51.
13 Kauffmann, S., Elliot, M. and Shmueli, D. 2013. Frames, framing and reframing. Available: www.beyondintractability.org/essay/development-conflict-theory
14 Chong, D. and Druckman, J. 2008. Framing theory. *Annual Review of Political Science*, 10: 103–126.
15 Albert, I. 2007. Reconceptualising electoral violence in Nigeria. In: I. O. Albert, D. Marco and V. Adetula, eds. *Perspectives on the 2003 elections in Nigeria*. Abuja: IDASA and Sterling- Holding Publishers.
16 Meadow, R. 2009. Political violence and the media. *Marquette Law Review* (online), 93 (1): 231–240.
17 Bilefsky, D. 2008. Violence Erupts in Macedonian Election. *N.Y. TIMES*, June 2.
18 Stremlau, N. and Price, M. 2009. *Media, elections and political violence in Eastern Africa: towards a comparative framework* (online). Oxford: University of Oxford Press. Available: http://global.asc.upenn.edu/fileLibrary/PDFs/PostelectionViolencereport.pdf

19 Ibid., 18
20 Hoglund, K. 2009. Electoral violence in conflict-ridden societies: concepts, causes, and consequences. *Terrorism and Political Violence*, 21: 412–427.
21 Orji, N. 2013. Making democracy safe: policies tackling electoral violence in Africa. *South African Journal of International Affairs* (online), 20 (3): 393–410.
22 Berman, B. 2010. Ethnicity and democracy in Africa. *JICA-RI Working Paper*, 22: 1–37.
23 Eifert, B. Miguel, E. and Posner, D. 2010. Political competition and ethnic identification in Africa. *American Journal of Political Science,* 54 (2): 494–510
24 Huber, J. 2012. Measuring ethnic voting: do proportional electoral laws politicize ethnicity? *American Journal of Political Science*, 56 (4): 986–1001.
25 Ehinmore, O. and Ehiabhi, O. 2013. Electoral violence and the crisis of democratic experience in post-colonial Nigeria. *Journal of Arts and Humanities (JAH)*, 2 (5): 46–51.
26 Douma, P. 2006. Poverty, relative deprivation and political exclusion as drivers of violent conflict in Sub-Saharan Africa. *Journal on Science and World Affairs*, 2 (2): 59–69.
27 Sambanis, N. 2004. *Poverty and the organisation of political violence: a review and some conjectures.* New Haven, CT: Yale University.
28 Fjelde, H. and Østby, G. 2011. Economic inequality and inter-group conflicts in Sub-Saharan Africa, 1990–2008. Paper prepared for the *conference on "Inequality, Grievances and Civil War" in Zurich, 10–12,* November 2011.
29 Chua, Amy. 2018. *Political tribes: group instinct and the fate of nations.* New York: Penguin Press.
30 Chua, Amy. 2018. The Destructive Dynamics of Political Tribalism. *The New York Times* (online), Available: www.nytimes.com/2018/02/20/opinion/destructive-political-tribalism.html (Accessed 29 September 2018).
31 Matei, F. 2013. The media's role in intelligence democratization. *International Journal of Intelligence and Counterintelligence* (online), 27 (1): 73–108.
32 Ibid., 46.
33 Ojwang, B. 2009. The semantics of peace and the role of the print media in the 2007–2008 post-election violence in Kenya. *Africa Media Review*, 17 (1): 23–50.
34 Stremlau, N. and Price, M. 2009. *Media, elections and political violence in Eastern Africa: towards a comparative framework* (online). Oxford: University of Oxford Press.
35 Duyile, D. 1987. *Makers of Nigerian press.* Lagos: Gong Communications.
36 Olayiwola, R. 1991. Political communications: press and politics in Nigeria's second republic. *Africa Media Review*, 5 (2): 31–45.
37 Douma, P. 2006. Poverty, relative deprivation and political exclusion as drivers of violent conflict in Sub-Saharan Africa. *Journal on Science and World Affairs*, 2 (2): 59–69.

4 The need for Peace Journalism training

Introduction

Responsible media is characterised by reportage that is unbiased and devoid of unnecessary hype that attracts public attention with the sole objectives of making money. However, the current state of reportage in Africa is manifest in reportage mainly motivated by factors such as ownership, geopolitical location, and religious/ethnic inclination. In Nigeria, for example, the dominance of southern-based newspapers has meant that newspaper reportage of sociopolitical issues such as elections is often perceived as pro-south and anti-north.

Also, it is generally believed that the imbalance in the spread of newspapers in the country has led to the biased reportage of sociopolitical, sociocultural, and socio-economic activities in the north in general.[1] This bias, according to Akinfeleye, has made most Nigerians view media reportage with suspicion and question the veracity of information put forward by the media.[2] Often, sometimes without intending to, journalistic reportage have either led to conflicts or fuelled existing ones. The unfortunate Rwandan genocide gives credence to the immense influence the media wields in instigating violence in society. I consistently refer to the unfortunate Rwandan genocide in this book, because it was the first major motivation for me to pursue a degree in journalism. As a young man growing and hearing about the war and the role played by the media, I contended that if the media could partly cause and/or instigate such wanton destruction, it can also play a huge role in promoting peace and development.[3] Palluck akin the media's role in the Rwandan genocide as "the voice of the devil"; he believed the media incited the public into one of the most gruesome genocides in recorded history.

The African media has evolved over time into an essential ingredient in the quest for political rebirth of the continent and thus have assumed very important roles, sometimes oblivious to media practitioners. This, according to Foster is due to the media's huge role of shaping the opinion and attitude of people, especially in their capacity as voters and in their capability to remain non-violent before, during, and after elections.[4] This immense influence of the media requires that media personnel are trained in ways of reporting social issues in a conflict-sensitive and responsible manner.

According to Lynch and McGoldrick, few journalists have been trained in the area of conflict analysis and theory. Thus, they are not well equipped to report issues that have consequences for societal peace. Training of journalists in conflict-sensitive reportage is imperative because journalists covering conflict are inescapably involved in the events and processes they are reporting on whether they like it or not. Conflict-sensitive reportage training of journalists is extremely crucial particularly in a volatile nation like those found on the continent of Africa. An informed understanding of conflict leads us to expect that statements put out by parties to a conflict will also be part of that conflict. Without this expectation, journalists may become stuck in what they termed, "the reality-based community," oblivious to the way realities are being created around them, and indeed their (journalists) part in creating them.

Peace Journalism training is beneficial to journalists because it will equip journalists with the skills to deliberately find ideas for non-violent responses from everywhere in society and bringing them to public knowledge. There is never, in any conflict, any shortage of non-violent responses, and it is the duty of the journalist to focus on them. In the words of the distinguished peace researcher John Paul Lederach,

> I have not experienced any situation of conflict, no matter how protracted or severe, from Central America to the Philippines to the Horn of Africa, where there have not been people who had a vision for peace, emerging often from their own experience of pain. Far too often, however, these same people are overlooked and disempowered either because they do not represent "official" power, whether on the side of government or the various militias, or because they are written off as biased and too personally affected by the conflict.
>
> (Adapted from Lynch and McGoldrick, 2005: 18)

I am persuaded that with the proper training, journalists can champion positive social change, particularly peaceful non-violent elections. For instance, the recent success of the 2013 election in Kenya has been severally attributed to the commendable role played by the media. The

International Crisis Group claim that the Kenyan media were not prepared for post-election violence that rocked the country shortly after the 2007–2008 elections. The media communicated in ways that suggested partisanship. Even worse is the fact that most vernacular radio stations were unwittingly used by politicians as a tool for disseminating hate speech that polarised the nation. However, the media played a more responsible role in the 2013 general elections by reporting the election in a way that fostered peace among Kenyans.

Determining journalists' training needs

It is common for Peace Journalism practitioners and trainers to "storm" Africa with the intention of conducting one interventionist training or the other. During the run-off to elections in most African countries, it is common to see training and retraining programmes organised for journalists on how to report elections in an "internationally acceptable" manner. Laudable as these efforts are, they nonetheless often raise several pertinent questions such as How are journalists' training needs determined? Are the training programmes designed in such a way as to take into cognisance the peculiar sociocultural and sociopolitical milieu of the journalists? Or, is there an assumption that journalists' training needs are the same everywhere, or is the decision to train reached methodically?

One of the most common mistakes international organisations conducting Peace Journalism training make is to assume that they know the training needs of journalists. This supposition often leads to intervention programmes that do not meet their immediate needs. In cases where the participants do not express their resentment, the trainer unwittingly leaves with the impression that he/she has achieved the set goal aim. In this section, I present practical steps that can be taken to determine journalists' training needs. The steps are drawn from my experience of conducting Peace Journalism training in Nigeria.

Owning the process

During my Peace Journalism training experience (discussed extensively in Chapter 5), I applied the action research methodology to conduct my study. The reason was simply that I wanted to be directly involved with the journalists in such a way that they would not feel schooled but actually feel like part owners of the entire process. One of the major standout differences between action research design and other research designs is the fact that it is participatory in nature, and it involves the voluntary participation and collaboration between the researchers (or trainers) and participants. This active participation by participants (in this case journalists) gives them a sense of ownership of the process, thereby making them more susceptible and amenable to change. Creating a feeling of ownership involves recognising that within political, economic, and social contexts, people are social beings. It also involves acknowledging that participants are contributors to the success or failure of the process and not just subjects of research.[5]

Anderson suggests that although the purpose of training is ultimately to teach people new ways of doing things, it should not be limited to that.[6] He suggests that training must also seek to build on what people already know. Proactive training deliberately seeks out new ways of helping people leverage on positives they already possess with the aim of further encouraging an improvement in the quality of their contribution to their organisations and communities. When the training need is collaboratively decided upon, the sustainability and adaptability to the new knowledge will be ensured. Training in traditional journalism is often limited to gathering and disseminating news to the public. Renowned peace journalists Howard is of the view that training in traditional journalism has not included the study of how best to cover violent conflict and has ignored any understanding of violent conflict as a social process.[7] Often, it is required that that journalist have knowledge, expertise, and experience, such as reporting on business and economics, public health, music, sports, or other topics. But the dynamics of violent conflict, like those that occur during electoral violence—its instigation, development, and resolution—are not much understood by most journalists nor proficiently reported on.

The need for introspection

In determining the training needs of journalists, I had to undertake a content analysis of the selected participants' past media reportage of sensitive issues. I also did a generic content analysis of newspaper reportage of social issues in Nigeria and how it has adversely affected the polity. An example that readily comes to mind is the unfortunate crisis that rocked the Northern Nigerian city of Kaduna in 2002 during the botched Miss World pageant. After six days of violent protests in Kaduna, an estimated 250 lives were lost.[8] Salawu recounts that the pageant that was scheduled was violently disrupted owing to a media report that pitched Christians against Muslims in Nigeria's restive Kaduna state. A style writer with *Thisday Newspaper*, one of Nigeria's leading dailies, had written a feature article published on 16 November 2002 in which she made an infamous comment that resulted in widespread violence, in a state already subtly divided along ethno-religious lines. The reporter stated that

> The Muslims thought it was immoral to bring 92 women to Nigeria to ask them to revel in vanity, what would Mohammed think? In all honesty, he would probably have chosen a wife from one of them.
>
> *(Thisday Newspaper*, 16 November 2002)

Suffice to add that before the article, there had been growing discontent, particularly among Nigeria's northern Muslims against the planned pageant. Expectedly, given the already tensed Muslim–Christian relationship in the state, the story did not go down well with the Muslim population who accused the newspaper of deliberately denigrating the Prophet Mohammed and Islam. Hence, they resorted to violent attacks on Christians and churches, killing, maiming, and burning. The fact that the reporter did not take into cognisance the volatile nature of religious discourse in Nigeria and the already tensed sociopolitical state of the nation at that time is proof of a dearth of or lack of adherence to conflict-sensitive journalism practice. Lynch and McGoldrick advocated for a paradigm shift for journalists. They remark that to pull off this sleight-of-hand about what to report, how to report it, are commonly disguised as natural and obvious.

Another sad aspect of the conflict was in the way it was reported by the Nigerian media. The reportage, rather than attempt to calm already tensed nerves, seemed to arouse the possibility of a reprisal attack from other sections of the country. The crisis came at the peak of the implementation of the Sharia penal code by certain states in Northern Nigeria. Newspaper reportage of the planned implementation of Sharia divided the country along ethnic and religious lines; even journalists were not spared the overt polarisation. For example, southern-based newspapers, mostly owned by Christians, were critical of the move, while newspapers based in the north, and mostly owned by Muslims, were pro-Shari'ah in their reportage. The 12 and 18 December 2002 editorials of the *New Tribune Newspaper*, a southern-based newspaper, gave a clear indication of the polarised nature of media reportage in Nigeria. The newspaper overtly opposed the planned introduction of Shari'ah and called on the government to stall the process. The paper condemned the fatwa (death sentence) imposed on the style editor who purportedly wrote the article that ignited the conflict.

The ideological inclination of any newspaper in Nigeria can easily be deconstructed. Most newspapers, their reporters, and editors overtly display ethnic and religious prejudice in their reportage. Hence, at the peak of the agitations for the implementation of the Sharia law by most of Nigeria's northern states, it was not surprising that most of the southern-based Nigerian newspapers did not support it. Prominent journalists like Ado-Kurawa believe that newspapers from the mainly Christian south consistently presented their position as civilised and the supporters of the Sharia as uncivilised and barbaric.[9] He summarised newspaper reportage of the Shari'ah crises thus:

> In the main, I think most of the anti-Shari'ah apostles have not shopped for new arguments and attitudes. More troubling is that they have not been totally honest about their grouse. Rather than let everybody know that their position is influenced either directly or remotely by a religious ideology; they pretend a certain hatred for barbarism or a passionate love for humanity. The religious or worldly ideology under which they hide has their own share of barbarity and inhumanity in the view of others.[10]

While Ado-Kurawa's views on the role played by the southern newspapers during the planned full implementation of the Shari'ah in Nigeria are debatable, one fact remains that most of the newspapers had (still have) southerners as their owners and southern Christians as their editors-in-chief. This undeniably had an impact, albeit subtly on the slant and tilt of the reportage of the Shari'ah crisis. Building journalists' Peace Journalism capacity is crucial when one considers that reporters as humans are vulnerable to emotional responses to social issues and may unwittingly lace their stories or features with emotive sentiments capable of inciting violence. Journalists' ethno-religious preferences have the tendency to come in the way of their professional or responsible reporting during conflicts. In the case of Kashmir, the Indian media reportage generally reflects considerable similarity to India's official position on the dispute. Likewise, in Pakistan, while religiously inspired terrorism has emerged as the most potent national security threat, those reporting and analysing it, or offering their opinions in the media, do so only in a reactive manner.

There is a need for journalists to be trained in the area of writing editorials that will engender peace rather than instigate violence. Editorials are arguably one of the most potent avenues through which the press can influence public discourse and ultimately set agenda.[11] An editorial is an official position by a media organisation concerning a particular policy, action, or idea. It is the logical perception of the newspaper on a social issue, often laced with the proprietor's thoughts or views for the purpose of persuading the readers (audience) to kick against an idea, a policy, or an action based on facts available. One of the biggest problems plaguing traditional journalists is that they lack the capacity to report the ever-changing conflict environment. Due to a lack of or insufficient conflict-sensitive reportage training, journalists find themselves ill-equipped to address the important social issues that demand so much of their attention.

Peace Journalism training for journalists is hinged on the belief that well-trained journalists will inevitably present news stories that are accurate, reliable, well contextualised, and responsible. Howard affirms that when journalists' capacities are built, they become strengthened and able to deepen the information and debate on social issues in ways that help citizens make inform sociopolitical decisions.

Training needs assessment survey

An important way to determine the training needs of participants is by conducting a training needs assessment survey in other to ascertain, from the participants, the areas they need capacity building. This is very crucial when one considers that training must be reinforced continually through consistent self-examination. This "self-examination" involves the extraction of meaningful data about the need for training from the journalists. The purpose of the survey is to determine what training needs to be developed to help individual journalists and their media organisation accomplish their goals and objectives, while also achieving the underlining aim of instilling the tenets of Peace Journalism to the journalists. The assessment will look at journalists' current knowledge, skills, and abilities to identify any gaps or areas of need. Once the training needs are identified, they will be developed in line with the objectives of the training. These objectives will form criteria for eventual evaluation of the training's impact.

An adequate training programme depends on securing reliable data as a basis for answering the following important questions:

- Who is in need of training?
- What areas of their professional life need a capacity building?
- Who is to be the training facilitator?
- How will the training be conducted?
- How will the training be evaluated for impact and effectiveness?

Peace Journalism training helps journalists treat conflict sensitivity in reportage as an important aspect of their work as journalists.

Notes

1 Ado-Kurawa, I. 2001. *Shari'ah and the press in Nigeria – Islam versus Western Christian Civilization*. Kano: Kurawa Holdings Limited.
2 Akinfeleye, R. 2003. Fourth estate of the realm or fourth estate of the wreck: imperative of social responsibility of the press. Being an Inaugural Lecture Delivered on Wednesday May 14, 2003, University of Lagos Main Auditorium.
3 Palluck, E. 2009. Reducing intergroup prejudice and conflict using the media: a field experiment in Rwanda. *Journal of Personality and Social Psychology*, 96: 574–587.
4 Foster, S. 2010. *Political communication*. Edinburgh: Edinburgh University Press.
5 McDonald, C. 2012. Understanding participatory action research: a qualitative research methodology option. *Canadian Journal of Action Research*, 13 (2): 34–50.
6 Anderson, G. 1994. A proactive model for training needs analysis. *Journal of European Industrial Training*, 18 (3): 1–22.
7 Howard, R. 2009. *Conflict-sensitive reporting: state of the art a course for journalists and journalism educators*. Place de Fontenoy: UNESCO.
8 Salawu, A. 2013. Recall of politics of identity in the narratives of the Nigerian press. *Journal of Communication*, 4 (1): 41–48.
9 Ado-Kurawa, I. 2001. *Shari'ah and the Press in Nigeria – Islam versus Western Christian Civilization*. Kano: Kurawa Holdings Limited.
10 Ibid., 89.
11 Duyile, D. 2005. *Writing for the media – a manual for African journalists*. Lagos: Gong Communication.

5   Bringing Peace Journalism to journalists engaged in reporting elections in Nigeria

An action research case study

Introduction

During the run-up to the 2015 general elections in Nigeria, there was widespread trepidation within and outside the nation that the increasing cases of electoral violence and political intimidation in the country would snowball into full-blown violence and possibly plunge it into civil war. This fear was largely influenced by the 2011 election, which was marred by pre- and post-election violence. Human Rights Watch (2011) estimated that the violence led to over 800 deaths in three days of rioting which engulfed parts of Northern Nigeria. Since the First Republic elections in the early 1960s, the Nigerian media has been very involved in the political process[1]. The diverse nature of the media makes its ideological inclination easy to decipher, because of reportage that is often tilted along ethnic and religious lines. Using data obtained through participatory action research involving 40 purposively selected participant journalists, this chapter draws from a published article detailing my PhD experience. It proposes an alternative method of news reportage using the Peace Journalism model. First coined by Johan Galtung, but fostered by Lynch and McGoldrick, the model encourages journalists to report social issues in ways that create opportunities for society to consider and value non-violent responses to conflict, using insights from conflict analysis and transformation to update concepts of balance, fairness, and accuracy in reporting. It also provides a new route map which traces the connections between journalists, their sources, the stories they cover, and the consequences of their reportage.

The problem

Nigeria's media has the potential to be divided along ethnic and religious lines. Given that most Nigerians view political aspirants in terms of their ethnic and religious background rather than their political ideology, and since most Nigerians rely on the media for information, there is often the tendency to fall prey to biased and insensitive reportage capable of inciting violence. This means that the majority of the populace are frequently vulnerable to prejudiced information which is often subtly presented as news, features, commentaries, documentaries, and so on. This problem formed the major motivation behind this research which aimed to build, through training, the capacity of the media to report elections in a conflict-sensitive manner.

Study objectives

Desirous of implementing an intervention that will mitigate the problem stated above, the following objectives were put forward for the study:

i   Determine the media's current mode of operation as regards election reportage in Nigeria;
ii Examine the extent to which media may be responsible for electoral-related violence in Nigeria;
iii Determine the training needs of media personnel particularly as regards conflict-sensitive reportage;
iv Implement training to enhance the media's capacity to operate in a way that discourages violence;
v   Carry out a preliminary evaluation of the outcome of the training.

The action research approach

This research was equally motivated by the "successful" outcome of the 2013 general elections in Kenya where the media played a key role in preventing violence. The International Crisis Group (2013) argues that the Kenyan media were not prepared for the post-election violence that rocked the country shortly after the 2007–2008 elections[2]. The media then communicated in ways that suggested partisanship. Even worse was the fact that most vernacular radio stations were unwittingly used by politicians as a tool for disseminating hate speech that polarised the nation. However, the media played a more responsible role in the 2013 general elections by reporting the election in a way that promoted peace among Kenyans. Thus, seeking, as it does, to evaluate the potential of training journalists on conflict-sensitive reportage as a way of fostering non-violent elections in Nigeria, this study is oriented within an action research paradigm. Action research is a research type that is focused on communities; it was first applied to improve conditions and practices in the health-care industry and is now commonly used in the social sciences and, in particular, peace research. The purpose of undertaking action research is to bring about change in specific contexts. In their systematic review of action research, Waterman, Tillen, Dickson, and Koning provide a comprehensive and practically useful definition:

> Action research is a period of inquiry, which describes, interprets and explains social situations while executing a change of intervention aimed at improvement and involvement. It is problem focused, context-specific and future-orientated. Action research is a group activity with an explicit value basis and is founded on a partnership between action researchers and participants, all of whom are involved in the change process. The participatory process is educative and empowering, involving a dynamic approach in which problem-identification, planning, action, and evaluation are interlinked. Knowledge may be advanced through reflection and research, and qualitative and quantitative research methods may be employed to collect data. Different types of knowledge may be produced by action research, including practical and propositional. The theory may be generated and refined and its general application explored through cycles of the action research process.[3]

A mixed research method was adopted for the study. This research method is appropriate because a single approach is limited to investigating phenomena in social science that are tightly enmeshed. Thus, by combining qualitative and quantitative research, there is a greater possibility of understanding human nature and reality.

Stages of the intervention

Action research normally cycles through the following phases: identifying a problem that needs intervention; collecting, organising, analysing, and interpreting data; and taking action based on this information. As earlier stated, action research is a way of analysing a social system and generating knowledge about it with the aim of changing it. This attempt at changing social systems can be achieved by following a set process. The different stages of this process were systematically followed in the study and are discussed below:

- Problem identification

The success of any action research is dependent on deciding from the start the main problem the research hopes to provide an intervention for.[4] The first step in any research study is deciding exactly what to study. Given that the main aim of action research is to effect change in a given situation, it becomes important to first identify the situation that requires change. Problems cannot be solved unless they are first identified and defined. Recognising the problem occurs when a situation is observed, and there is an acknowledgment that things could be done better. It also involves seeking to understand the nature of the situation and discovering the possible causal factors. Effectively identifying the problem helps in the formulation of the research questions for the study. For example, why do journalists report the way they do? What factors influence journalists' styles of reportage? Does journalistic reportage affect the outcome of elections?.

One of the ways this research sought to identify the problem was by finding out the current mode of reportage by journalists in Nigeria. This was a major objective of the study. To achieve the aim, pretraining questionnaires were administered to the participating journalists. From the findings obtained through the pretraining questionnaire, it was discovered that the dominant writing style of the participating journalists was traditional (war) journalism which often subtly instigates violence. The journalists averred that they would report any news story as long as the sources were "verifiable" which clearly showed a lack of conflict-sensitive reportage knowledge.[5] McGoldrick believes reporting issues simply because they are "verifiable" could be risky for societal peace because politicians and government sources often skew stories in their favour and unwary traditional journalists often do not take the time to delve into the "why" of issues. The problem with this lack of focus on the "why" of conflicts is that without some exploration of the underlying causes of conflicts, they can appear, by default, as the only sensible response to disagreements.

Findings from the study also showed that journalists often hinge their practice of traditional (war) journalism on the need to be "objective." The most used word all through the training was objectivity; journalists regard it as the most important tenet in the journalism profession. According to McGoldrick, the traditional news brand of objectivity inadvertently makes the media the battlefield for opposing politicians who struggle to make their points clear in a tug-of-war style, thereby further heating the polity rather than ameliorating the situation. Thus, it was clear from the pretraining questionnaires that journalists were in dire need of conflict-sensitive journalism training.

• Data gathering

After clearly identifying the problem, the next stage of the research was the collection of data that aided the design of an appropriate intervention. Information gathering in the case of this research involved simply interacting with journalists, media owners, and/or politicians in the research area with the aim of gauging their perceptions of the proposed research problem. In order to get relevant data that would help attain the research goal, decisions had to be made about the appropriate data collection instruments and techniques that would be used in the study.

Fraenkel and Wallen suggest three main categories of data collection techniques.[6] Although their suggestions were directly meant for action research in an educational setting, they have profound applicability in peace research and were applied in this study. First, they suggest a process of observation of participants involved in the study. In the case of an educational setting, they state that these participants might include students, other teachers, parents, and administrators. In order to describe what is being seen and heard, they suggested researchers use field notes or journals to record their observations. In the case of this study, the researcher had to observe the participating journalists by spending some time with them at their various newsrooms. By observing their news reportage style, the researcher was able to understand some of the remote factors influencing their style of news dissemination.

Second, they suggest the use of interviews to collect relevant data for the study. The researcher interviewed management and staff of the Nigerian Union of Journalists (NUJ) and facilitated focus group discussions during the training. The interactions emanating from the various focus groups were analysed using elements of conversation analysis, which is the study of talk in interaction and examines conversation as the action taking place between actors.[7] The goal of analysing focus groups using conversation analysis is to understand how society produces orderly social interactions through laid down methods and processes.

Third, Fraenkel and Wallen recommend the analysis of existing records as another way of gathering data for action research. They believe that it is convenient considering that it is often the least time-consuming since the data have already been collected. The responsibility of the researcher is to make some sense of what is already there. A few examples of this type of data include attendance records, minutes of meetings, newspaper features, policy manuals, editorials, and so on.

Given that people generally get excited after training sessions and often make positive affirmations regarding positive change in behaviour (in this case reportage), it becomes important to conduct a content analysis of the participants' reportage after the training in order to determine whether or not they actually implemented what they learned in the training in their day-to-day reportage. As stated earlier, the analysis of data was done in two parts—analysis of the pre- and posttraining questionnaires and analysis of media produced by the participating journalists. The stories were to be analysed to see how many applied the 17-point plan for practical Peace Journalism put forward by Lynch and McGoldrick (see Chapter 8 for a detailed discussion on the 17-point plan).

- Data interpretation

Once the data have been obtained, the next important step is to analyse the data in order to arrive at a reasonable conclusion that will guide the direction of the research. A number of relatively user-friendly procedures can help a practitioner identify the trends and patterns in action research data. During the process of analysing data, the researcher will be able to identify the major "story" told by the data and why the story played out in that particular way. Analysing data can help the action researcher acquire an improved understanding of the occurrence under investigation and, as a result, can help in formulating the necessary interventions. Utilising the findings of the analysis of the data obtained from the pretraining questionnaire and content analysis, the researcher designed a training manual on conflict-sensitive reportage of elections which was used to train participating journalists.

- The intervention

The aim of action research is primarily to take action or intervene when a problem has been identified and sufficient relevant data have been obtained. Before action is taken, the researcher determines whether or not the data collected answer the research questions. In order to preserve the cyclical nature of action research, it is important to effectively monitor, evaluate and revise the process during the implementation process of the action plan.

- The training

The main objective of the training was to equip journalists with the basic conflict-sensitive journalism skills that will empower them to cover election processes in a fair, balanced, and non-partisan way. This would then encourage a culture of non-violence and enable citizens to become well-informed, interested, and active participants in the country's political decision-making processes. To aid in the facilitation of the training process, a manual was designed by the researcher. The manual was made up of three modules. The first module focused on helping participants understand the concept of conflict, its causes and effects, and how they can manage or avoid it through their reportage. The expected outcome of the module included the following:

- A clear understanding of the term conflict, the causes of conflicts, and conflict management techniques.
- The relationship between journalists' reportage and societal peace or conflict. The expected qualities of a journalist with respect to impartiality, accuracy, and responsibility.

The second module focused on introducing participants to the Peace Journalism model. The expected outcome of the module included the following:

- A clear understanding of the term "Peace Journalism."
- An understanding of the differences between traditional (war) journalism and Peace Journalism.
- A detailed exploration of Lynch and McGoldrick's 17-point plan for Peace Journalism.

Module 3 focused on training journalists in the process of election reportage. The expected outcomes included the following:

- Helping journalists clearly identify the important issues that need their attention during the electoral process and the professional way of covering it.
- Equipping them with the skills to be fair, impartial, and objective in their reportage.
- Building their capacity to sensitise the public on the need to be peaceful and non-violent throughout the electoral process.

For each of the modules, participants were broken into five groups consisting of eight journalists in each group. The manual contained icebreakers that required journalists to deliberate in groups after which their responses were captured on a flip chart. The researcher, along with the co-facilitators, trained journalists on the dynamics of conflict.[8] Drawing from Lynch and Galtung extensive work, it was explained that when people, groups, and even countries are in conflict, often due to the incompatibility of goals, there is a clear and present danger of violence. Journalists were then trained to use conflict situations as stepping stones to transform the conflict in ways that create opportunities for peace in society.

- Evaluation

When interventions are carried out in action research, it is always very important to determine whether or not the interventions had any meaningful impact. Project evaluation is an important element of the action research process since it is an opportunity to "stand back" and reflect on the intervention that has been carried out and write down observations that will aid the process of strategising.[9] Evaluation is consistent with the cyclical representations of action research. Each cycle is required to conclude with phases of monitoring and reflection that seek to ask the following questions:

- What effects have my actions had?
- How does this relate to what I wanted to achieve?

Sincere answers to the above questions will help the researcher understand his/her results from the intervention. According to Townsend, evaluation is concerned with trying to untangle what has been learned from the process of intervention and to judge whether it is adequate for the desired change process.[10] It also raises questions about what should come next, this could mean further investigation of the context or nature of the practice or make changes to its design.

- Outcome evaluation

In order to ascertain the impact the training had on participants, the researcher distributed a posttraining questionnaire. The outcome of the training was also determined through a content analysis of the journalists' reportage after the training.

The posttraining questionnaire was administered a month after the first training. This was to allow the researcher enough time to observe the journalists at their work and also to provide sufficient time for the journalists to implement ideas that were presented during the training sessions. The questions and responses are discussed below.

Question 1: In what ways will your practice change as a result of the training?

As earlier stated, the major aim of the study is to help journalists report social issues better by being more conflict sensitive in their reportage. Even though the researcher planned to undertake a content analysis of the participants' reportage after the training, he still sought to find out from the journalists the specific ways in which they thought their reportage would change as a result of the training.

The responses obtained were as varied as the participants; however, some points were common to all respondents. For instance, all 40 journalists affirmed that they would shun ethnic and religious bias in their reportage. They said that they would put the peace of the nation first ahead of ethnic and religious affiliations. This response is heart-warming when one considers that a large percentage of conflicts in Nigeria have their roots in ethnicity and religion. The polarised nature of Nigeria's society is further heightened and energised by the tainted and skewed lens of ethnicity and religion as portrayed by media owners and practitioners.

Question 2: In what specific way(s) do you think your reportage will foster peaceful elections?

Most of the respondents stated that they would apply Lynch and McGoldrick's 17-point plan for practical Peace Journalism in their reportage. Five points stood out:

- Most of the journalists stated that they would avoid the conflict-inducing attitude of portraying a conflict situation as a "battle" between only two parties whose sole aim is to win over the same goals. In this case, the two parties would be politicians or political parties seeking to attain the single goal of a political position. Journalists stated that they would focus more on issues and how these issues affect the generality of the population.
- The participating journalists also said that they would apply Lynch and McGoldrick's suggestion that journalists should endeavour

to ask questions that may reveal areas of commonalities between conflicting parties instead of focusing on that which divides. According to Lynch and McGoldrick, this helps the parties to realise that they actually have goals that are both compatible and shared.

• Journalists also said that they would desist from reporting violent acts and describing horrific scenes. They said they would change their approach by showing people's delay struggles with frustration and depravity.

• Interestingly, journalists stated that they would make adjustments in their choice of language and tones. They said that they would avoid words such as "devastated," "defenceless," "pathetic," and "tragedy."

Instead, they stated that they would apply the skills garnered through the training. Journalists stated that they would instead report on what has been done and could be done by the people.

• Journalists also said they would avoid using demonising labels such as "terrorists," "extremist," "fanatic," and "fundamentalists." Instead, they stated that they would henceforth call people by the names they give themselves. Lynch and McGoldrick advised that precision should be applied when describing subjects or objects in a story, for example, "bombers," and "suicide hijackers." According to them, these words are less partisan and give more information.

Challenges, unexpected outcomes, and limitations

There are uncertainties in research which are almost inevitable. Participants may back out from the research, key interviewees may not show up, government policies and regulations may change thereby hampering the research process, themes may emerge during discussions or training that may sway the direction of the research, and so on.

My original research plan was to conduct another set of training a few weeks before the 2015 general elections in Nigeria to serve as a refresher course for the participating journalists. However, I had to cancel the training because of my inability to obtain an extension for my student's visa on time. The unexpected situation meant I had to communicate with the participants online and I also had to track their bylines online. This was very difficult considering that most newspaper outfits in Nigeria do not have active archives.

One other major unexpected twist was the shift in the discussions from being primarily about elections, to other social concerns. During the training period, journalists wanted to know how Peace Journalism can be applied to stem the scourge of terrorism which was at its peak in Northcentral Nigeria at that time. The timeliness of the issue meant that the training was adjusted a bit to accommodate ideas and techniques of conflict-sensitive reportage that would aid in ending terrorism as perpetrated by Boko Haram.

Chapter summary: project outcome

Throughout the course of the training implementation and analysis of data, several themes emerged. First, journalists were unanimous in their position that they indeed have the "power" to nurture a culture of peace in the society. However, they also asserted that they often act as muffled drums because of the overbearing influence of media owners and draconian government policies. Thus, in order not to offend media owners and also in a bid to avoid government clampdown, journalists have fallen prey to a practice of journalism that is devoid of conflict sensitivity. One of the goals of the training was to hand "power" back to the journalists; the power to influence society positively by setting a positive developmental agenda for public discourse.

Second, journalists were of the opinion that the poor remuneration, which is a common problem among Nigerian journalists, makes them easy prey for politicians courting favourable coverage and makes it difficult for them to be objective and non-partisan in their reportage.

Third, adequate training and retraining of journalists have a great positive impact on their reportage style, particularly their conflict-sensitive reportage of sociocultural and sociopolitical issues. It was observed through the content analysis of the journalists' reportage after the training that the journalists applied the tips they got from the training to their journalistic practice and determinedly sought ways through which they could advocate for peace through their reportage. It was also clear that journalists applied their gate-keeping skills in giving newsworthiness to stories that engendered peace, thereby setting an agenda for peace as a public discourse.

Notes

1 Human Rights Watch, 2011. World Report 2011: Nigeria *Events of 2010.* Available: https://www.hrw.org/world-report/2011/country-chapters/nigeria
2 International Crisis Group, 2013. Kenya's 2013 Elections: *Preparations for elections in Kenya turn into high gear today as the parties in the three major coalitions nominate their candidates.* Available: https://www.crisisgroup. org/africa/horn-africa/kenya/kenya-s-2013-elections

3 Waterman, H., Tillen, D., Dickson, R. and Koning, K. 2001. Action research: a systematic review and guidance for assessment. *Health Technol Assess.* 5 (23): iii–157.
4 Johnson, A. 2011. *A short guide to action research.* 4th ed. Boston, MA: Allyn and Bacon.
5 McGoldrick, A. 2006. War journalism and objectivity. *Conflict and Communication* (online), 5 (2): 1–7.
6 Fraenkel, J. and Wallen, N. 2003. *How to design and evaluate research in education.* New York: McGraw-Hill.
7 Silverman, D. 2006. *Interpreting qualitative data.* 3rd ed. Thousand Oaks, CA: Sage Publications.
8 Lynch, J. and Galtung, J. 2010. *Reporting conflict: new directions in peace journalism.* St. Lucia: University of Queensland Press.
9 Lienert, T. 2002. Doing action research evaluation. *Stronger Families Learning Exchange Bulletin,* 1 (1): 16–20.
10 Townsend, A. 2013. *Action research: the challenges of understanding and changing practice.* Berkshire: McGraw-Hill.

6 Journalists' responses to Peace Journalism

Introduction

Chapter 3 demonstrated a clear link between media reportage and electoral violence, as was seen in Kenya where media instigated post-election violence in 2007 led to the death of about 1,300 people and the displacement of close to 600,000 others.[1] No doubt, the post-election violence that overwhelmed Kenya further shows that the media is indeed a two-edged sword and that its effect depends to a large extent on whoever wields it. Thus, it is pertinent to ensure that media personnel are trained on how to report using the Peace Journalism (PJ) mode—in ways that engender peace and non-violence.

Considering that the mass media have the ability to effectively enlighten people, Utor accords the mass media the duty of decision moulder and "society's teacher."[2] The media have evolved over time into an essential ingredient in the process of political rebirth in many nations. By virtue of this responsibility, the mass media helps to shape the opinion and attitude of people, especially in their capacity as voters and in their capability to remain non-violent before, during, and after elections. The best way to ensure productivity, quality of media output, and effectiveness of media personnel is through the consistent capacity building, improvements in quality and access to facilities and equipment, new media, and means of and advocating adherence to ethical practices of journalism agreed upon by the media professionals themselves.

Does PJ work?

Lynch is of the opinion that convention seems to have governed most journalistic work today.[3] He remarks that since speed is essential in the journalistic practice, formulating responses to breaking news would be near-impossible from its first principles, starting afresh every time.

Conventions can be challenged and supplemented if journalists and civil society combine their self-awareness and efforts at reforms and collectively push forward the idea that PJ can indeed work if given its pride of place in society.

Lynch and McGoldrick argue that the PJ model does really work. In order to proffer proofs of the efficacy of PJ as a tool for promoting peace in the society, they conducted a series of studies in four countries—Australia, the Philippines, South Africa, and Mexico. In each of these countries, the duo produced a total of 42 television news packages (two versions each of 21 stories), one an unedited "regular" news story, while the other versions were skewed to have elements of PJ inserted into the news stories. Both versions were subsequently played to over 550 participants. The positive feedback they got from their study confirmed their view that PJ does work, no matter how little the effect. Their findings are presented below.

The Australian study: from anger to empathy

The Australian study conducted by Lynch and McGoldrick focused on the most pressing social theme in Australian news—the handling of the ever-increasing case of asylum seekers. The public seems often to take the brunt of the claims and counterclaims from opposing political parties on the issue. Expectedly, when participants at the workshop organised by Lynch and McGoldrick were played a standard news package, based on opposing views from the political divides, the major reaction was anger aimed at the perceived "other side" of the argument from the respondent's point of view. Lynch and McGoldrick remark that what is often missing in traditional journalism is a content that is people centred.[4] This is where PJ differs from war journalism because whereas war journalism is elite oriented and focuses on males who are able-bodied, acts as their spokesperson, and provides names of perceived evil-doers, PJ differs in that its focus is on all forms of sufferings, no matter who is involved, giving a limelight to peacemakers and providing a voice for the voiceless in society.

Lynch described the impact the people-oriented content of their adjusted version of the asylum seekers story had on participants thus:

> For our adjusted version, then, we included an interview with a refugee, Ali Jafari: a Hazara man who'd fled Afghanistan by boat and successfully settled in Australia. This awoke people's empathy, and now the anger tended to be directed towards the iniquitous system in which people like Mr. Jafari are locked up for

long periods waiting for their claims to be processed. And there was a notably increased appetite for hearing about suggestions for change: the "solution orientation" that is another key aspect of PJ.

The Philippines: shows of strength- versus solution-oriented news

The Philippines has had a long drawn battle between the Communist Party of the Philippines and the government of the Philippines. While talks were ongoing on the possibility of ending the protracted conflict that had beleaguered the nation, the National People's Army (NPA) set landmines, while the Armed Forces of the Philippines made high-profile arrests in "dawn raids." This, unfortunately, threatened to scuttle the ongoing peace process. News reportage of the peace process did not inspire confidence in the populace. Most viewers lost hope of a possibility that the problem could be solved with many even stating that what the nation needed was an intensified military suppression. Sensing that public dissatisfaction was growing at a fast pace, a PJ version of the same issue was aired. The new version contained interviews with a prominent leader of the NPA, Ka Oris, in Mindanao and gave background information on why people join the organisation. The news also provided exhaustive backgrounding and context on the remote and immediate causes of the conflict.

Lynch and McGoldrick described the impact the PJ story had on the public thus:

> The peace journalism news also featured pictures of a peace rally, and heard from a local Protestant Bishop, and two Indigenous, or "Lumad" leaders, on what they wanted to come out of the talks. Justice, in respect of deprivation and disenfranchisement, was the dominant theme of their "wish-list." Viewers were now much more likely to favour holistic solutions, with optimism that peace could be produced, again with the proviso that Philippines society must be made fairer and more inclusive if the roots of the problem were to be adequately addressed.

By shifting focus from victory orientation of war journalism to solution orientation of the PJ which brought peace initiatives to the public fore, mitigates the possibilities of more war, focuses on structure, peaceful society and cultural heritage, there was a renewed belief in the minds of members of the public about the possibilities of a peaceful resolution to the protracted conflict.

South Africa: "Turning a Corner" from a rape case

Lynch and McGoldrick report that at the time of their study in South Africa, the dominant news was the horrendous incident in which a gang of young men raped a disabled young woman, recorded it, and posted it on the Internet. As expected, the heinous crime generated an unprecedented public outcry. Expectedly, news reports concerning the incident were mostly reactive and focused only on the visible effects of the violence meted on the young woman. In a bid to mitigate the situation, a PJ version of the narrative was produced to provide the society with all sides of the story.

In contrast to the war journalism that was the norm in South Africa during the period, the PJ version of the news played to participants in the study had an interview with Dumisani Rebombo, an activist and educator with *Sonke Gender Justice*, a Johannesburg-based non-governmental organisation (NGO). It was a deliberate "turning of a corner" aimed at providing viewers with actors of peace.

Lynch and McGoldrick report the effect this had on participants thus:

> He told us how, over three decades ago, he too had taken part in a gang rape, considered an "initiation ceremony" among his teenaged peers. Years later, he'd sought out the survivor of the attack and begged her forgiveness. She set one condition: make sure neither you nor your son, ever does this to anyone again. At this, Dumisani began running workshops, drawing on his experience to challenge men and boys about their attitudes to women. Viewers of the PJ version were just as horrified, and felt just as sorry for the young woman who'd suffered the gang rape, as the WJ viewers. But they were less likely to "externalize" the problem: to blame "them down there" for doing it and to regard punitive responses as representing a solution. And they were significantly more likely to accept that a single incident of direct violence is constructed by many contributory factors of structural and cultural violence (albeit none of them put it in quite those terms!) It is, therefore, implicitly incumbent on everyone to think what they themselves may be able to contribute to addressing those factors, as Dumisani had done.

As can be observed from the remarkable story of Dumisani, by focusing on positive peace efforts in the society, peace journalists were able to shift focus from the impact of violence to the solution to violence, that way, peace journalists encourage the proactive mindset that seeks ways of improving society.

Mexico: PJ and the "war on drugs"

The drug law that ravaged Mexico under President Felipe Calderon was threatening to destabilise the country. The intensified "war on drugs" declared by the President had left as many as 60,000 casualties in six years.[5] The tension in Mexico at the peak of the "drug war" put enormous pressure on the President who was about to conduct an election. Also, media reports were awash with the rising death toll from the resultant chaos, and it seemed that there was no respite in sight. In the Mexican study, a PJ version of the happenings in the country deliberately focused on success stories and agents of change rather than the rising death figures and combating drug lords.

For the PJ version of the continuing drug war, interviews were conducted with members of the public who were actually doing something about the drug problem that plagued the country. Eduardo Galloy Tello who had lost his daughter to the drug war advocated a regulation of drugs in such a way as to make it lose its market value and subsequently drop down the price, thereby making it less attractive to criminals. Likewise, the interview was conducted with Erik Ponce, a young man who was rescued by a local community centre from a life of drugs and is now studying music at university.

Lynch and McGoldrick were of the opinion that ending the terrible violence could only be achieved when young men like Erik are provided with opportunities to tell their sides of the story and work for peace. This is part of what is known as peace with justice and widely understood by viewers of the PJ version of the story. After conducting successful PJ research in four countries, they concluded thus,

> Our research shows that peace journalism works. It does indeed prompt its audiences to make different meanings about key conflict issues, to be more receptive to nonviolent responses. At a time when fears are being expressed that commercial funding models will be unable to sustain good journalism, which is an invitation to non-commercial funders to step in. And if they sponsor initiatives in peace journalism, they can be confident, on the basis of our findings, that they will be making an important contribution to societal resources for peace.

PJ training and the reportage of elections: case studies

* Kenya: When journalists decided to "Write Right."

The 2007 post-election violence is still fresh in the memories of most Kenyans. The preventable loss of lives and property and the hundreds of thousands of displaced people as a result of the violence was tied to several factors, including the ever-vociferous Kenyan media. According to the International Crisis Group (2013)[6], Kenyan media were not adequately prepared for the 2008 post-election violence that affected the country. This unpreparedness was evident in their inability to communicate the election results and the violence that ensued afterward without prejudice. The vernacular radio stations were the worst culprits; rather than work for peace, they incited the public against one another by overtly taking sides with politicians and deliberately providing them with the medium with which to disseminate hate speech. However, the media played a more responsible role in the 2013 general elections by reporting the election in a way that fostered peace among Kenyans. Unlike the 2007 general election that polarised the Kenyan public along ethnic lines with the media acting as the battlefield, the 2013 election saw a major shift in the way the Kenyan media handled issues pertaining to the election.

Training and retraining programmes were conducted for journalists in Kenya in a bid to forestall a recurrence of the unfortunate violence that engulfed the country in 2008 that was regrettably linked to unprofessional media reportage. For example, the Peace Journalism Foundation (PJF), an East African-based peace media NGO with the aim of creating a peaceful society through the media conducted training for Kenyan journalists in the run-off to the elections. The training was facilitated by the Director of the Centre for Global Peace Journalism at Park University in Parkville, Missouri, Prof. Steven Youngblood.

Given that vernacular radio programmes were severally accused of hate speech that incited the public into violence, one of the focus areas of the training included training presenters into taking charge of phone-in programmes on radio and also in-studio guests to avoid public incitement and/or the spread of hate speech. Print journalists, on the other hand, were trained on the need for vigilance regarding the content of their news so that they do not unintentionally incite the public into violence. Also, print journalists were trained to be vigilant about the news content before publishing so as to ensure that their stories are balanced and provide opportunities for all relevant voices to be heard rather than focusing only on politicians.

Similarly, several other organisations such as the International Media Support Group conducted training for Kenyan journalists with the aim of ensuring that they were safe during elections and also that they are able to provide balanced and fair reportage through a journalism style that is conflict sensitive. The journalists were also provided with access to trauma counselling. More than 200 journalists in hot spots most prone to violence were trained by the Media Council of Kenya in collaboration with various stakeholders. It is important to state that the while the 2013 general election in Kenya cannot be said to be perfect (I believe that there are no perfect elections), it is, however, a marked improvement from the 2007 election that was marred with violence. The media, a major perpetrator of the 2008 post-election violence played a more responsible role this time by mobilising and sensitising the public towards peace and non-violence. It will be imprudent to completely attribute the peaceful election in Kenya to media reportage; however, the fact remains that the media played a very significant role and much of this was achieved through effective training of journalists on conflict-sensitive reportage.

Zimbabwe

Zimbabwe was also swept by a wave of pre- and post-election violence in 2008 during presidential and parliamentary election similar to what happened in during the 2007 general election in Kenya. The election, which pitched the incumbent, President Robert Mugabe of the Zimbabwe African National Union-Patriotic Front (ZANU-PF), Morgan Tsvangirai of the Movement for Democratic Change (MDC), and Simba Makoni, an independent candidate turned violent when the MDC candidate refused the accept the election result. Although the media was not directly accused of inciting the public into violence as it occurred in Kenya, Mutanda remarks that the government-controlled media, *The Herald*, instigated violence in the country by labelling members of the rival MDC as violence perpetrators.[7] The 11 April 2001 edition of *The Herald* commented thus, *"the MDC is provoking violence and this should be nipped in the bud before it develops further like it did in last years' parliamentary elections ...."*

According to Mutanda, the media was vehement in its effort to disparage opposition politicians and stalwarts by using manipulative overtones seeking to gain legitimacy in the face of a dwindling electorate. The MDC and its stalwarts were portrayed as a puppet party of the West because of its known links with countries in Western Europe. In order to prevent a repeat of the 2008 electoral violence in Zimbabwe, the Zimbabwe Electoral Commission (ZEC) with the assistance of the Electoral Institute for Sustainable Democracy in Africa (EISA) organised a media training workshop for local journalists in the country with the aim of equipping them with the necessary skills need for conflict-sensitive reportage of elections. The idea to engage the media regularly emerged during ZEC's Strategic Plan consultative workshops where the media was identified as one of the key stakeholders in the electoral process. The media thus plays an important role in educating and informing the public about the electoral process. ZEC also has the mandate to monitor the coverage of elections by the media in accordance with the provisions of Statutory Instrument 33 of 2008.

It can be argued that the impact of the training on the election was evident in the peaceful and non-violent manner in which the election was conducted. The Zimbabwean media was largely responsible and unbiased in its reportage, and this played a huge role in ensuring that the Zimbabwean public remains peaceful despite misgivings in some quarters regarding the conduct of the elections. The connection between provocative media and electoral violence has been established in numerous places around the world. Kenya, Zimbabwe, Ghana, Nigeria, and so on have experienced electoral violence connected to inciting media. Likewise, the connection between non-violent elections and responsible peace-oriented media has been established in countries such as Ghana, Kenya, and Zimbabwe which have experienced non-violent elections credited to responsible media reportage.

The extensive research conducted by Lynch and McGoldrick (2012) across four nations—Australia, Philippines, South Africa, and Mexico—proved the efficacy of PJ training on journalists reportage of sensitive social issues such as elections and on peace in the society. PJ does not overwrite conventional journalism; it encourages its audience to be receptive to non-violent responses to conflicts by making different meanings about key conflict issues. I am of the opinion that PJ as a model for responsible journalism can only be imbibed by journalists through consistent training and retraining.

Notes

1 Youngblood, S. 2012. Heated elections test peace journalists. *The Peace Journalist* (online), 1 (2): 1–24. Available: www.park.edu/peacecenter
2 Utor, M. 2000. The mass media, ethics and professionalism in Nigeria. *Journal of Mass Communication and Society*, 1 (2): 1–17.
3 Lynch, J. 2007. Peace journalism and its discontents. *Conflict and Communication Online* (online), 6 (2): 1–13. Available: www.cco.regener-online. de/2007_2/pdf/lynch.pdf
4 Lynch, J. and McGoldrick, A. 2005. *Peace Journalism*. Stroud: Hawthorn Press.
5 Lynch, J. and McGoldrick, A. 2012. Peace journalism works. *The Peace Journalist* (online), 1 (2): 1–24. Available: www.park.edu/peacecenter
6 International Crisis Group, 2013. Kenya's 2013 Elections: *Preparations for elections in Kenya turn into high gear today as the parties in the three major coalitions nominate their candidates.* Available: https://www.crisisgroup. org/africa/horn-africa/kenya/kenya-s-2013-elections
7 Mutanda, D. 2012. The local media and Zimbabwe's land reform program. *Journal of Sustainable Development in Africa*, 14 (3): 262–279.

7 Journalism or advocacy? Understanding the limits of Peace Journalism

Introduction

In 2008, the nation of Kenya teetered towards war rising from the political violence that greeted the general elections. Although several factors have been adduced for Kenya's propensity towards violence during elections, the role of the media seems to be recurrent with every general election. For example, as has been severally mentioned in this book, the media was partly accused of instigating the violence that led to the death of close to 1,000 Kenyans and the displacement of thousands of others through hate messages. In a reportage style akin to that employed during the ill-famed Rwandan genocide of 1994, the Kenyan media pitched the country's different ethno-religious groups against each other. This resulted in the wanton loss of lives and property, as well as a very volatile sociopolitical climate. Thus, by 2013, when the country was about to conduct another general election, apprehension was very high among the populace. Many feared the factors that fuelled violence in the previous elections had not been addressed and that a repeat, or even worse possible scenario, was assured. However, in what seemed like a sharp deviation from what transpired in 2008, media reportage of the election was more conflict sensitive. Although there were irregularities, the 2013 election recorded less violence, and the media was lauded as a key reason for that. In the 2017 election, however, the media was once again at the centre of public discourse. This time, the media was accused of "sacrificing democracy" at the altar of peace. Public watchers accused the media of downplaying irregularities and outright rigging of the elections. This chapter examines Peace Journalism (PJ) in its many complexities and contextual dynamics, with a bid to make the thin line between PJ and advocacy clearer.

Like Kenya, like the rest of Africa

I chose the Kenyan election as a case study for this chapter, and indeed this book, because Kenya has had three elections in the last decade, with the media playing very key and active roles in all of them. This is unsurprising, considering that Kenya has a very vibrant media which is often regarded as one of Africa's most vociferous.[1] The country boasts of a vibrant media landscape, including over 200 radio and TV stations. Radio remains the key media and most accessible source of information, with television, the Internet, and social media growing rapidly, especially for urban populations. However, powerful private media houses with links to the country's political elite still dominate the media sector. From the early days of British formed newspapers such as the *Taveta Chronicle* which was established in 1895 by Rev. Robert Stegal of the Church Missionary Society (CMS), to the establishment of the *Leader* by the British East African Company in 1899, the media has played active roles in setting agenda for public discourse in the country either serving as a device to maintain the status quo by legitimising the rights of the colonial government or in later days as a tool for social rebirth and the promotion of human rights, as well as the provision of forums for public debates.

It is also important to state that Kenya has experienced serious outbreaks of politically motivated violence at each of the elections from 1992 onwards (1992 marking the resumption of multiparty elections after a gap of 29 years), during the attempted coup against President Daniel Arap Moi by air force officers in 1982 and during the 2005 referendum campaign.[2] Violence has also punctuated disputes over land ownership, political patronage, and historical grievances derived from the upheavals of the colonial period (for more detailed examinations of these issues, see Somerville, 2011)[3]. But the ferocity, rapid escalation, and scale of the violence after the 2007 election took many Kenyans and international observers by surprise, shattering myths of Kenya as an essentially politically stable country (*The Guardian*, 31 December 2007; *Financial Times*, 29 December 2007; and *Independent*, 6 January 2008 all have variants on the—haven of stability descends into violent chaos—approach to reporting the violence). The conflict that ensued after election results were announced was due in part to the ethnic, religious, and tribal nature of Kenyan politics and in many ways due to uncontrolled media reportage.[4] The violence was hastened by heightened expectations, hyped pre-election opinion polls, and media reports of alleged rigging.

In the run-up to the 2007 general election, the Kenyan public depended on the media for information regarding the electoral process and candidates involved. To the media's credit, it provided live up-dates at the national vote tallying centre and set the tempo of pub-lic interest as a national conflict unfolded amid finger-pointing and showboating by political-party loyalists. However, in discharging its duties, the media wittingly or unwittingly incited the Kenyan public to violence, with attendant avoidable loss of lives and property.[5] Radio broadcast shortly after the election contributed in no small measure in fuelling the post-election violence that rocked the country. It can be argued that the major culprits were the vernacular radio stations which broadcast in *Luo, Kikuyu, Kalenjin,* and other local languages. The stations overtly broadcast hate messages similar to those trans-mitted during the unfortunate Rwandan genocide. The mainstream English media seemed obliged to remain unbiased as its messages were largely objective, while the vernacular stations fuelled the embers of hatred and divisions.

The "organised, deliberate and intentional" nature of the hate-filled media messages suggested that they were not just errors by a few jour-nalists or a spontaneous outburst of anger; the messages were in fact targeted at perceived political and ethnic "enemies." The target was clear—others'. The aim? A clearly well-thought-out orchestrated vio-lence with the sole aim of grabbing political position, which in most of Africa often translates to economic power. According to Somerville, most of the radio stations broadcasting in *Kalenjin, Luo,* and *Kikuyu* deliberately and intentionally increased ethnic suspicion, directly ad-vocated violence against other ethnic groups, and disseminated mes-sages of hatred and incitement.[6] Before long, media messages at the peak of the run-off to the elections drew unfortunate comparisons with what was obtainable during the Rwandan genocide of 1994. The *IPS News Service* described the situation in Kenya thus:

> The media was partly blamed for the Rwandan genocide 14 years ago which left nearly one million people dead in 100 days. "Kill the Inkotanyi [cockroaches]!" a local radio station urged its listen-ers at the time. "30 Days in Words and Pictures: Media Response in Kenya During the Election Crisis"—a workshop organized here last week by California based media advocacy group Internews—enabled media professionals to conduct a "self-audit" of the role local media played in the postelection violence. The audit revealed that media—especially vernacular radio stations—might be partly to blame for the on-going violence sparked off by the announce-ment of Mwai Kibaki as the winner of the Dec. 27 elections.
>
> (IPS, 2 February 2008)

The choice of radio as a means for disseminating messages (in this case, hate messages) is due in many ways to its affordability, portability, and wide reach. Radio is widely listened to in Kenya, as in most African countries, and the expansion of FM stations in 2002 following Kenya African National Union's (KANU's) electoral defeat, further expanded Kenya's media's space and further broadened radio's influence and impact. The country experienced rapid expansion in the number of FM stations broadcasting in *Kikuyu, Kalenjin, Luo,* and *Luhya.*[7] Somerville recalls that *Kass FM* became the most influential Kalenjin station, while *Lake Victoria FM* and *Ramogi FM* were the leading Luo stations. They were criticised by human rights groups during the 2005 referendum campaign for inciting political violence—*Inooro FM* was pro-Kibaki and broadcast songs deriding—beasts from the West, meaning Odinga and his supporters (KNHCR, 2007). The Kibaki government briefly suspended *Kass FM* in November 2005, accusing it of inciting violence during the referendum campaign—Odinga supporters accused the government of attacking *Kass* because it was independent of the government and broadcast the views of Odinga supporters opposed to the planned new constitution. *Kass* was allowed to resume broadcasting when it produced transcripts of programmes and succeeded in proving that no hate messages had been broadcast. This gave the station greater credibility among Kalenjin listeners and increased suspicion of the Kibaki government (Somerville, 2010).

Thus, when it was time for the 2013 general elections in Kenya, public apprehension was expectedly high as many were not sure whether or not the election would be characterised by the violence of past elections. Given that the media was partly blamed for the violence that marred the 2008 elections, many wondered what role the media was going to play this time around.[8] Training and retraining programmes were conducted for journalists in Kenya in a bid to forestall a recurrence of the unfortunate violence that engulfed the country in 2007. For example, the Peace Journalism Foundation (PJF), an East African-based peace media non-governmental organisation (NGO) with the aim of creating a peaceful society through the media, conducted training for Kenyan journalists in the run-off to the elections. Similarly, several other organisations such as the International Media Support Group conducted training for Kenyan journalists with the aim of ensuring that they were safe during elections and also that they are able to provide balanced and fair reportage through a journalism style that is conflict sensitive. It is important to state that although the 2013 general election in

Kenya was not in any way perfect, it was a marked improvement from the 2007 election that was marred by violence. The media, a major perpetrator of the 2008 post-election violence played a more responsible role this time by mobilising and sensitising the public towards peace and non-violence.

The 2013 election provided an opportunity for alternative election reportage. The local media in Kenya displayed extreme caution and restraint, bordering on self-censorship, in terms of how it reported the election. Acts of violence and disturbances in some parts of the country during the election were downplayed, perhaps in the belief that reporting these events might trigger reprisal incidents elsewhere or make the violence appear more widespread than it really was. The Kenyan media had decided not to "disturb the peace," even if it meant under-reporting electoral misconduct. In some regards, one may argue that the Kenyan press practised PJ during the 2013 election, renowned PJ scholar and trainer, Steven Youngblood, does not think so. He contends that the media's under-reportage of issues during the election negates the principles of PJ. He further argues that if media in Kenya or elsewhere are ignoring or minimising news (in the excuse of promoting peace), then they are not practising PJ or any real journalism for that matter. This "peace messaging" was also premised on the awareness that a politically unstable Kenya was not good for local businesses and foreign investors and that remaining peaceful or non-violent was good for the economy. In the long run, the election was largely free of violence (at least overtly and directly). Suffice to add that the Kenyan election was not without its criticisms. Critics believe the media, in an attempt to avoid a possible repeat of the electoral violence that rocked the country in 2007 practice a journalism of "compromise." The general elections gave Kenyans an unsatisfactory choice between the half-truths of the foreign press and the illusions of their own national media.

In 2017, Kenyan had another election. Like the elections of 2008 and 2013, the media played a very active role before, during, and after the electoral process. The election would go down in history as one of the most contentious, not only in Kenya but across the African continent. Although eight candidates, including three independent aspirants, vied for the presidency, it was clearly a contest between incumbent President Uhuru Kenyatta of the Jubilee Party of Kenya and Mr. Raila Odinga of the National Super Alliance (NASA). The media's role in the election once more brought to the fore the contestations regarding PJ's propensity to unwittingly slide into advocacy. Renowned peace journalist, Steven Youngblood, described the media's reportage of the election and its (mis)representation of PJ thus:

> Nowhere in the theories of peace journalism elaborated by its founders, Dr. Johan Galtung, Dr. Jake Lynch, and Annabel McGoldrick, and nowhere in my new university textbook *Peace Journalism Principles and Practices*, does anyone say that peace journalists should ignore the unpleasant and potentially volatile news. "Tension and protests" are newsworthy, and must be covered. Election rigging is news, and cannot be ignored by real journalists. Peace journalism does not question if these stories should be reported but instead asks how journalists should cover this news. Do we report responsibly and in a manner that does not incite violence, or in ways that fuel the fire and exacerbate an already tense situation?
>
> (Youngblood, 2018)

The Kenyan media reportage of the 2017 election was PJ in intentions but traditional reportage in principle. I contend, like Youngblood, that if in a bid to promote "peace" we foster injustice, we have actually done more disservice to society.[9] It is important to note that in reporting sensitive issues like elections, too much or even too little information can indeed be a dangerous thing. The media, by focusing on the manifestations rather than the causes of conflict, does not tell the full story. Such forms of misreporting give rise to misconceptions that only add fuel to already existing fire(s) of mistrust and ethnic suspicions. I draw out lessons that are accruable from the Kenyan experience for journalists reporting elections in other countries on the continent and/or globally.

What PJ is not: lessons from the 2017 Kenyan elections

PJ scholars and practitioners are often accused of being in the defensive by default. It seems, by default, PJ scholars are expected to be "armed" with counter-responses or proofs to support PJ's effectiveness or relevance to society, especially as it concerns societal peace. It also always seems like "they" are constantly explaining what PJ is while hoping that the audience and/or readers will figure out what PJ is not. One of PJ's leading proponents, Jake Lynch, posits that journalists' dislike for PJ stems from the fact that it "forces" a critical self-awareness of journalistic structure and agency inscribed in PJ's analysis and methods. This, according to Lynch, is tantamount to a rejection of some key propositions from scholarship on journalism and communications, established by researchers over several decades. Since contestations about what PJ is, have not reduced divergent, and sometimes antagonistic opinions, perhaps a discourse of what PJ is not could provide a better understanding of the model. Nowhere, in recent times, have PJ's tenets been questioned like the 2017 Kenyan elections, and I hope to show through content analysis of selected newspaper stories that emanated from the country pre-, during, and post-elections, what PJ is not.

1 PJ is not a conscious disparaging of journalistic objectivity

A major criticism of PJ is that it inhibits journalists from practising fair and objective reporting. Fairness and objectivity, critics argue, are the universally known and accepted tenets of the journalism profession. Without objectivity, many believe, journalism loses its respect. However, objectivity without sensitive reportage can often be the bane of journalism. As Lee points out, objectivity is possibly one of the biggest obstacles to journalists playing a more responsible and beneficial role in public life.[10] Objectivity, by emphasising facts and overt events, devalues ideas and fragments experience and make complex social phenomena more difficult to understand.[11] There are certain positive connotations associated with the term "objectivity," such as fairness and the pursuit of truth without favour. However, objectivity is not fixed; it is relative because whether or not objectivity is a desirable and achievable goal for reporting in a democratic society is a debatable question.

In the wake of the prolonged and highly contested 2017 Presidential Elections in Kenya, there has been an intense debate within the media, political, and other circles about the role(s) the media played in the elections. The major debate has revolved around whether or not the media lived up to the public expectations on reporting the entire election process accurately, in depth, fairly, and in a manner that offered adequate space to the contesting parties, especially the two major fiercely competing political formations—NASA led by Raila Odinga and the Jubilee Party led by Uhuru Kenyatta. The latter was eventually declared the winner after a controversial repeat election on 26 November 2017. The debate is whether or not the media served the broader national good, identifying and prioritising key national issues and presenting, analysing, and projecting them in a manner that helps in the country's democratic transformation and in conflict resolution.

Shortly after the results of the 2017 general elections in Kenya were released, the leader of the opposition party NASA, Raila Odinga, rejected and challenged the results, leading to a boycott of the repeat elections of October 2017 ordered by Kenya's courts. Mr. Odinga cited several irregularities as reasons for his and his party's positions, including media bias which was evident in deliberate misinformation, downplaying of violent attacks on his supporters, and under-reportage of his party's activities. He thereafter threatened to establish a "people's assembly," to carry out protests and boycotts, while seeking changes to the constitution. In an 11 August 2017 column in the *Washington Post*, Patrick Gathara, a renowned Kenyan journalist, activist, and cartoonist, recalls that in the run-up to the election, there was great public resistance to "preaching peace" as a means of pre-empting violence in the event that the election was disrupted. The media, in a bid to preach "peace," created a fear of possible anarchy in the minds of Kenyans and wittingly or unwittingly made a deal with the government based on a mutual interest in plundering the public. While PJ seeks to promote public knowledge and understanding of alternatives to violence as means of resolving differences, it nonetheless does not mean that the public should not be made aware of the "whole story" in news items. Withholding or "hiding" stories in the guise that it can potentially instigate public violence is in itself a form of violence. Deliberate misinformation or concealment of information is violence; for ignorance can breed deadlier forms of violence.

In the days leading up to the announcement of the result, there was palpable tension in the country as the Independent Electoral and Boundaries Commission (IEBC) delayed the announcements of the results, leading to the outbreak of violence in some parts of the country, especially in Nairobi and some other urban centres. The violence, which started small and with little or no violence, soon snowballed into clashes with the police, leading to the death of at least seven people, with many sustaining various degrees of injuries. According to Gathara, one would not know about the incidence of watching most Kenyan media. There seemed to have been a deliberate attempt to conceal the stories so as to prevent spiral effects and reprisal attacks in other regions of the country. By deliberately under-reporting or completely shutting out the pockets of protests in the country, especially in the capital, the media sacrificed "telling all sides of the story," which is a major tenet of PJ, for subtle advocacy, which PJ is not.

Part of PJ's tenets is the intentional analysis of conflict in such a way as to create open spaces, which provide opportunities for the exploration of the causes and outcomes of conflicts, thereby making them more transparent. In order words, PJ does not support the "hiding" of conflicts, but it actually exposes it, providing detailed background of various actors, third-party instigators/mediators, underlining motives, and so on, thereby helping the public have better understanding of what is at stake, who the actors are, and whether or not there are alternative conflict resolution mechanisms other than overt violence. This can only be achieved by giving voices to all parties involved in a contest (in this case, elections).

What transpired during the 2017 general election, however, was the opposite. During the announcement of results by the IEBC, the media took every result announced hook, line, and sinker without any attempt to independently verify.[12] McGoldrick describes this scenario as a bias for official sources. She remarks that news by its nature is change centred, yet its understanding of how change is attained is often one-dimensional. Thus, journalists often sometimes unwittingly favour realism and ignore insights of peace and conflicts which hold that conflicts can change in a number of ways, thereby negating the one-direction nature of news. However, because of the quest for news objectivity, we often hear so little about other actors of peace compared to official sources. The Kenyan media, it seemed, took the IEBC's result as final, without consciously verifying the authenticity of the result, and unfortunately silencing Raila Odinga's claims of irregularities. Many newspapers had the capacity to undertake independent verifications, but they did not take the route. In an address to the Senate, Samuel Macharia, owner of Kenya's largest TV and radio network, *Royal Media Services*, told Parliamentarians that his network had independently tracked results at every election since 1992, his group, however, did not take the path this time.[13] Instead, it joined other members of the press to crowd the national tallying centre in Nairobi, hanging on every word issued by the IEBC. The press was content with running its unofficial tallies, rather than get official counts and tallies from lower levels. Gathara described the situation succinctly:

> ... And worst of all, as the politicians and IEBC officials haggle in Nairobi over which numbers are correct, the media is happy to play along rather than spare us the drama by simply heading down to the 40,000 polling stations where, even now, the official and final results are posted outside for all to see.

2 PJ is not "Good News" journalism

There is a general belief that news is not news until it is bad. When back in the 1990s, the then BBC newsreader Martin Lewis suggested that news should move away from its traditional tendency to be commonly "bad" to a propensity for more good news stories on the TV and in newspapers; he was derided by his colleagues and, according to him, was even threatened with a sack by his employers. Recounting his experience years later, Lewis remarked thus,

> ... My job was on the line. I thought—"Here is an organization respected around the world, the bastion of democratic debate and argument and assumes the right—quite properly—to analyse and criticise every other sector in society, but they won't tolerate a public discussion about {how} they operate their own news business and indeed the news business itself".

Lewis' experience would be different today as many news organisations have started considering tilting their reportage towards "good" news over "bad" news. *DigiDay*, an online trade magazine which creates content, services, and community that fosters change in media and communication, reports that *Huffington Post*'s Good News has increased its traffic 85% over the last year and gets twice the social referrals of other *Huffington Post* content.[14] Given the growth of social media and its increasing importance as a veritable tool for business growth and development, one can safely state that good news is good business for *Huffington Post*. Other publishers of positive news aver that countering traditional media's penchant for bad news is not only good for good for societal well-being, but it also helps to catalyse potential solutions to the problems of society.

In many ways, during the 2017 general elections, journalists in Kenya intentionally or unintentionally practised "good journalism" and not PJ as many claimed. The media painted a façade of normality by ignoring or under-reporting citizens' protests and frustrations in order not to "disturb the peace." Most of Kenya's media saw the reportage of peaceful marches and public protests as "bad news" capable of painting the nation in bad light among the international community and also capable of initiating violence. The alternative?—report from the collation centre and give the impression "all is well." The problem with this type of conflating reportage is that it interweaves PJ with "good news" journalism and almost makes both seem one and the same. Truth is, they are not. The difference between the two lies in what is produced. While good news journalism focuses on the production and focuses on more "good news," PJ's focus is on the creation of more public awareness.

According to Ouma, the Kenyan mainstream media blacked out the clashes that transpired between state security agencies and sections of opposition supporters who were demonstrating against the disputed presidential results.[15] Although it must be said that several factors, such as the mysterious death of Chris Msando, the IEBC's IT boss, days before the elections, the crackdown on sections of "opposition-allied" observers and technocrats, and the vicious state crackdown on NGOs that contested the presidential results, contributed to the media blackout, it nonetheless does not change the fact that the media consciously downplay what they regarded as "bad" news in other not to inflame the already tension-soaked political milieu. Ouma further argued that the local mainstream media attempted to paint an image of a country that had "moved on" from the electoral conflict and rather focused on trivialities like "the Güntherian."[16] For instance, NTV presented "back to business" coverage and interviewed a number of pedestrians within Nairobi's central business district to demonstrate how "Nairobians return to work after the polls," so as "to maintain a facade of normality."

It is not advocacy

At the core of PJ's tenet is the belief that an aware member of the society would be able to make informed decisions on the best possible ways to resolve an issue. Such awareness includes the various actors involved in a given conflict or conflict situation, the possible unseen influencers, the people who benefit and those who stand to lose from a conflict, men and women who are working for peaceful resolution of the conflict, as well as creating awareness of the possible non-violent conflict resolution options available to all parties involved in the conflict. This involves not just reporting "good" news, or under-reporting "bad" news, it involves conscious engagement by the journalist in ways that gives them opportunity to understand contexts and backgrounds, which would ultimately help in providing detailed coverage or reportage of events in ways that present society with information of all sides and all angles of a social phenomenon.

However, David Loyn, one of PJ's fiercest critics, has always maintained that his discontent with PJ stems from where it puts the reporter. He argues that by demanding engagement from the reporter, PJ fails to recognise, or refuses to accept that there is no such thing as a transparent observer, the implied contract with the audience is that the standpoint of the reporter is at least an attempt to be an observer.[17] He remarks that

> Reporting news is about addressing the complications of a messy, visceral world and constructing a narrative, telling stories, not

"searching under stones." This may involve shining a light on some dark places, where the peace/solution-oriented seeker for conflict resolution would want to "frame" the situation in a different way. But if people are out to kill each other then, as journalists, we are not there to stop them.

I agree with Loyn's position that in an attempt to practice PJ, most "practitioners" often sometimes (un)wittingly apply a prescriptive set of rules that actually exclude the engagements that PJ claims to promote. PJ, according to Loyn, often comes from a single narrow point. He reckons that PJ should not give attention to "peace-makers" only, or go about looking for peacemakers (or in this context, good news), but they should instead go out in search of news, and when they find it, they should report it, without excluding anyone or anything, notwithstanding whether it is "good" or "bad." Where I disagree with Loyn is in his subtle disapproving of the need for the presentation of contexts and backgrounding in news stories, as suggested by peace journalists. I do not agree with Loyn that "our task is always to seek to find out what is going on, not carrying any other baggage." I think that journalists should not approach their tasks as detached neutral observers of social situations, for as Loyn himself alludes, journalists cannot be completely detached. While it may sound emotive and sentimental, the fact remains that journalists need to have at the back of their minds the possible impacts their reportage or a lack of it has on society. That is where the "peace" angle in PJ comes in. I agree with Lynch and McGoldrick that journalists hold the society a huge responsibility to provide ample contexts and backgrounding to their stories so that events would not be understood from a single point of view, and so that conflicts should not be reduced to events happening in the "now," without historical precedents.

Many argue that journalists in Kenya, like their counterparts in most part of the continent, face daunting tasks when it comes to discharging their duties. Some even argue that credit should be given to any journalist who reports at all, given the dangerous conditions they operate in. For example, a report by *Article 19*, an organisation committed to helping people (including journalists) express themselves freely and engage in public life without fear of discrimination, shows that journalists who covered the 2017 general elections worked in the exceptionally challenging environment. Many of them faced direct attacks, arrests, been denied access to areas, and receiving forms of threats, even more so after the August elections and in the run-up to the October repeat presidential polls.[18] While it is commendable that the media in Kenya took intentional and deliberate steps in consciously reporting in ways that sought to foster peace and non-violence during the 2017 elections, it is nonetheless important to note that deliberately avoiding or under-reporting news reports or events that deemed "bad news" negated their very effort. News should be served to the public as a buffet. Just like restaurants make an effort to let their clients know the ingredients in the buffet before them, journalists should endeavour to provide contexts and adequate backgrounding to their stories so that members of the society can decide what to do with the news before them, from an informed point of view. Like Kempf posits, "if peace journalism is understood the right way, it is not an antipode of good journalism, but its necessary prerequisite."[19]

One of the major challenges with practising PJ is that journalists could unintentionally delve into advocacy, and instead of informing the public, set out to advance an agenda—it does not matter whether or not the agenda is "good" or "bad."[20] When news items are critically examined, elements of advocacy ("support or argument for a cause") can be seen subtly "tucked-in" as by-products of the selective nature of journalism which leads to some voices and issues being included, ignored or promoted more strongly than others. Seth Ouma aptly describes Kenyan media's reportage of the 2017 general elections:

> Despite the largely positive coverage towards the 2017 elections, the Kenyan media later abandoned reporting for democracy during the tallying process when supporting calls for transparency was most critically needed. Besides, the local media failed to cover objectively the brutal clashes between state security agencies and opposition supporters under the pretext of concern for the country's stability. However, despite the need to promote stability, if reporting for democracy had been the local media's intended project, space was there for fair coverage of human rights abuses, as well as arguments for restraint. Instead, the local media switched to excessive peace-preaching amidst a clear attempt to sway the country away from the electoral conflict, by creating an illusionary "back to business" narrative. Whether this is the product of massive editorial political bias, journalistic vulnerability to personal financial pressures or simply a desire for a quiet life is hard to say. However, it is evident that this culminated in a betrayal of free speech through advocacy rather than analysis.

Notes

1 Republic of Kenya European Union Election Observation Mission FINAL REPORT General Elections 2017. Available: https://eeas.europa.eu/sites/eeas/files/eu_eom_kenya_2017_final_report_0.pdf

2 Somerville, K. 2010. Kenya: violence, hate speech and vernacular radio. *MIGS Occasional Paper*, 1–55. Available: https://migs.concordia.ca/documents/MIGSKenyaFinalEditMarch2010.pdf

3 Somerville, K. 2011. Violences et discours radiophoniques de haine au Kenya: Problèmes de définition et d'identification. *Afrique contemporaine*, no 240,(4), 125–140. doi:10.3917/afco.240.0125.

4 Ibid., 66.

5 Stremlau, N. and Price, M. 2009. *Media, elections and political violence in Eastern Africa: towards a comparative framework* (online). Oxford: University of Oxford Press.

6 Ibid., 1

7 Somerville, K. 2011. Violence, hate speech and inflammatory broadcasting in Kenya: the problems of definition and identification. *Ecquid Novi: African Journalism Studies*, 32: 82–101. Available: www.tandfonline.com/doi/abs/10.1080/02560054.2011.545568?journalCode=recq20

8 Laker, G. and Wanzala, O. 2012. Kenya journalists learn to speak, write peace. *The Peace Journalist* (online), 1 (2): 1–24. Available: www.park.edu/peacecenter

9 Singh, S. 2011. Peace journalism, media objectivity and Western news values in fragile Pacific island states: reflections from Pacific island journos. *The Journal of Pacific Studies*, 31 (2): 259–275. Available: https://core.ac.uk/download/pdf/11532623.pdf

10 Lee, S. 2010. Peace journalism: principles and structural limitations in the news coverage of three conflicts. *Mass Communication and Society*, 13: 361–384.

11 Ibid., 8.

12 McGoldrick, A. 2006. War journalism and objectivity. *Conflict and Communication Online*, 5 (2): 1–7. Available: www.cco.regener-online.de/2006_2/pdf/mcgoldrick.pdf

13 Gathara, P. Kenya's elections show how the media has sold its soul. *Washington Post*, August 11, 2017. Available: www.washingtonpost.com/news/global-opinions/wp/2017/08/11/kenyas-elections-show-how-the-media-has-sold-its-soul/?noredirect=on&utm_term=.a81805694ee6

14 Sahil, P. 2016. Huffington Post finds feel good videos perform best on Facebook, March 23, 2016. Available: https://digiday.com/media/huffington-post-finds-solution-oriented-videos-outperform-others-facebook/

15 Ouma, S. 2018. Reporting for democracy or convenience? The Kenyan media and the 2017 elections. *The Round Table*, 107 (2): 173–188

16 Ibid.

17 Loyn, D. Good journalism or peace journalism? – Counterplea by David Loyn. *Conflict & Communication Online*, 6 (2): 1–6.

18 Article 19, 2018. Kenya: violations of media freedom, May 2017–April 2018.

19 Kempf, W. 2007. Peace journalism: a tightrope walk between advocacy journalism and constructive conflict coverage. *Conflict & Communication Online*, 6 (2): 1–9. Available: www.cco.regener-online.de/2007_2/pdf/kempf.pdf

20 Fisher, C. 2016. The advocacy continuum: towards a theory of advocacy in journalism. *Journalism*, 17 (6): 711–726.

8   A 17-point plan for reporting African elections

Introduction

Africa has witnessed a surge in the rate and spate of "democratic elections" since the turn of the century. In their radical book *How to Rig an Election*, authors Brian Klass and Nic Cheeseman argue that one of the reasons elections have increased globally is because authoritarian leaders, especially those domiciled on the African continent, have devised new strategies of rigging elections in ways that are harder for members of the public to see. Thus, one can safely argue that although elections have increased on the continent, democracy cannot be said to have flourished in the process. Today, all across the continent, "former" dictators are allowing elections to take place in their countries. They win international acceptance and sometimes accolades for conducting elections, even though long before actual voting takes place, they put in place machinery to enable them to rig and get away with it. They use new technologies to hack elections and even sponsor and promote fake news. Unfortunately, many journalists have ended up as pawns in their hands and have aided the fostering of illegality, which has the potential to snowball into direct violence.

In this chapter, I attempt to present practical steps that journalists can take to ensure that they report elections from a Peace Journalism perspective, while not sacrificing journalistic integrity and professionalism. I have, with permissions, adopted Lynch and McGoldrick's 17-point plan for Peace Journalism, and I have attempted to contextualise it to African scenarios. The aim is to present workable suggestions for devising and applying such a strategy to re-balance the reporting of elections and intentionally countering the distorting influence of traditional journalism that is often partisan and inflammatory.

A 17-point plan for practical reportage of elections in Africa using the Peace Journalism approach

1   *AVOID* portraying every election as consisting of only two parties contesting for political positions with the only logical outcome been for one to win and the other to lose. *INSTEAD* disaggregate and pay attention to other "smaller" parties involved in the political process, thereby opening up more creative potentials for a range of outcomes. Ask yourself, which other political parties are involved in the process? Have they been given adequate attention too? Multiparty democracy is common in most African countries, but you would not know by reading or watching media reportage on the continent. All across the continent, elections have been reduced to two or three prominent candidates, with the others either underreported or not reported at all. In the 2017 elections in Kenya, the Independent Electoral and Boundaries Commission (IEBC) approved 66 political parties to contest various positions, with five of them presenting presidential candidates—Uhuru Kenyatta or the Jubilee Party, Raila Odinga of the National Super Alliance, Abduba Dida of the Alliance for Real Change, Ekuru Aukot of the Thirdway Alliance Kenya, and Cyrus Jirongo of the United Democratic Party. Three other candidates contested as independent candidates—Joseph Nyagah, Japheth Kaluyu, and Michael Wainaina. The media, however, reduced the entire process to an Uhuru versus Odinga affair, thereby unwittingly depriving Kenyans of options.

Like Kenya, the Nigerian media often reduces elections to two-party horse races. According to the Independent National Electoral Commission of Nigeria (INEC), there are 91 registered political parties in Nigeria, but in the run-up to the 2019 general elections, like previous elections, the focus has been on the All Progressives Congress (APC) and the opposition People's Democratic Party (PDP). Prominent, and sometimes more credible, candidates from other political parties do not get the attention they often deserve. Although the social media has helped these "other" candidates spread their reach, the fact remains that traditional media such as radio and newspapers still play very active roles in the political process, and their focus has always been on the so-called big political parties. The same scenario is obtainable in South Africa where the African National Congress (ANC), The Democratic Alliance (DA), and the Economic Freedom Fighters (the EFF) take a large chunk of media reportage. All over the continent, the scenario is similar—two or three "big" parties clutching all the media attention, while other "smaller" parties are overlooked. Journalists hold the society a responsibility of given substantial coverage to other parties and/or candidates so that the playing ground can be a lot more level.

2 *AVOID* accepting the stark distinction between "self" and "other"; these can be used to build a sense that another party is a "threat" or "beyond the pale" of civilised behaviour. Both are key justifications for electoral violence. Instead seek the "other" in the "self" and vice versa. It is common for candidates and political parties to engage in finger-pointing during the electoral process; the aim is always to appear before the electorate as the "better" of the "other," with the hope that it would translate into votes and/ or support. Lynch and McGoldrick advice journalists covering elections to go beyond these stark distinctions by asking certain pertinent questions such as: How different is the party's behaviour from that for which it ascribes to the "other"?

3 *AVOID* reporting an election as if it is only going on in the big cities. Journalists often focus their reportage of elections on happenings in the big cities such as Nairobi, Lagos, Accra, and Harare. The reasons may not be farfetched—most electoral management bodies have their headquarters in the big cities, the collation centres are also often cited in the nation's capitals, and most media outfits do not have the financial and human resources required to send reporters to hithermost parts of their respective countries. What this means is that oftentimes, riggings go unreported, and electoral manipulations and/or malpractices thrive unabated. The journalist reporting elections using the Peace Journalism approach should *INSTEAD* try to bring to the fore the electoral process and the people involved in other parts of the country, especially in the rural areas. Also, journalists should endeavour to ask the following questions so as to provide members of the society ample contexts to the entire electoral process. Ask:

- Who are all the people with a stake in the outcome of the election?
- How do these stakeholders relate to each other?
- Who gains from the conflict that may result from the process?
- What are they doing to influence the conflict? And so on.

4 When reporting electoral violence, *AVOID* assessing the merits of a violent action or policy of violence in terms of its visible effects only. *INSTEAD* try to find ways of reporting on the invisible

effects, for example, the long-term consequences of psychological damage and trauma, perhaps increasing the likelihood that those affected will be violent in future, either against other people or, as a group, against other groups or other countries.

5 One of the biggest challenges plaguing political parties in Africa is the lack of internal democracy. In most countries on the continent, there is centralised style of leadership in which the ruling party's National Executive Council or individuals dominate the party's decision-making process. Thus, bad decisions by the leadership are often unchecked within the party structures before they become public policy. Journalists covering elections or the electoral process must *AVOID* letting parties define themselves by simply quoting their leaders' restatements of familiar demands or positions. *INSTEAD*, they should enquire for themselves into goals, needs, and interests:

- How are people on the ground affected by the party's decisions in everyday life?
- What do they want to be changed?
- Who else is speaking up for them besides their political leaders? Answers to this are often surprisingly accessible, as even many small grass-roots organisations now have websites.
- Is the position stated by their leaders the only way or the best way to achieve the changes they want?
- This may help to empower parties to clarify their needs and interests and articulate their goals, making creative outcomes more likely.

6 *AVOID* concentrating always on what divides the political parties, on the differences between what each party says they want. *INSTEAD* try asking questions which may reveal areas of common ground, and leading your report with answers which suggest that at least some goals, needs, and interests may be compatible or shared. An example is the politicisation of the land question in South Africa.

The land question in post-apartheid South Africa is arguably one of the most contentious and sensitive issues in the country's sociopolitical milieu. The government's promise to undertake a concerted land reform programme aimed at historical redress, wealth redistribution, and economic growth has been disparaged by a section of the populace who are displeased by the policy's slow pace of implementation, the inability to translate redistributed land into improvements in agricultural productivity, and a top-down approach to land reform that is not people centred. Thus, whenever the delicate issue of land reform is discussed, emotional outbursts are common given the nation's peculiar sociocultural, socio-economic, and sociopolitical history.

One platform where the land reform discourse has generated much controversy is the media. South Africa's vociferous media has the potential to be divided along ethnic and racial lines. Media messages in South Africa often have a myriad of interpretations that may not necessarily be as intended by the source. Decades of racial segregation and economic inequality mean that media messages are often wittingly or unwittingly construed through a nexus of sociocultural, sociopolitical, ethnic, and racial connotations. Thus, since most South Africans rely on the media for information, especially regarding issues like land reforms, there is the tendency to fall prey to biased and insensitive reportage, capable of inciting violence which is elicited by prejudiced information often presented as news, especially during the electoral process, as land has become a major campaign theme in the country.

7 As stated in the previous chapter, not reporting a violent incident because of the fear of inciting reprisal responses is not Peace Journalism, it does not even qualify as good journalism. When incidences occur, it is the duty of journalists to report them as they happened, while providing ample context, and detailed background where they are available. Peace journalists covering elections, especially electoral violence, should, however, *AVOID* only reporting the violent acts and describing "the horror." If you exclude everything else, you suggest that the only explanation for violence is previous violence (revenge); the only remedy, more violence (coercion/punishment). *INSTEAD* show how people have been blocked and frustrated or deprived during the electoral process, as a way of explaining how the conditions for violence are being produced.

8 When reporting electoral manipulations or violence, *AVOID* blaming a particular political party for "starting it." It is common to find political parties pointing fingers at opponents and accusing them of starting the violence. Sadly, the media sometimes falls prey to this gimmicks and (un)intentionally "join sides," thereby aggravating the conflict. Journalists who find themselves in such situations should *INSTEAD* try looking at how shared problems and issues are leading to consequences which all the political parties say they never intended.

9 *AVOID* focusing exclusively on the suffering, fears, and grievances of only one party. This divides the parties into "villains" and "victims," and suggests that coercing or punishing the villains represents a solution. This scenario plays out in most elections on the continent of Africa. The ruling party is always often described as perpetrators of violence and/or electoral manipulation during the electoral process. The truth, however, is that most times all the parties involved in the process directly or indirectly instigate their members to violence and also take part in electoral manipulations. Journalists should *INSTEAD* treat as equally newsworthy the suffering, fears, and grievances of all parties.

10 When reporting disagreements or violence during the electoral process, it is important to *AVOID* "victimising" languages such as "devastated," "defenseless," "pathetic," and "tragedy" which only tell us what has been done to and could be done for a group of people by others. This is dis-empowering and limits the options for change. *INSTEAD* report on what has been done and could be done by the people. Do not just ask them how they feel; also ask them how they are coping and what they think. Can they suggest any solutions?

11 *AVOID* the imprecise use of emotive words to describe what has happened to people, such as the following:

- "Genocide" literally means the wiping out of an entire people—in United Nations (UN) terminology today, the killing of more than half a million people.
- "Tragedy" is a form of drama, originally Greek, in which someone's fault or weakness ultimately proves his or her undoing.
- "Assassination" is the murder of a head of state.
- "Massacre" is the deliberate killing of people known to be unarmed and defenceless. Are we sure? Or do we not know? Might these people have died in battle?
- "Systematic"—for example, raping or forcing people from their homes. Has it really been organised in a deliberate pattern, or have there been a number of unrelated, albeit extremely nasty, incidents?

INSTEAD always be precise about what we know. Do not minimise suffering but reserve the strongest language for the gravest situations or you will beggar the language and help to justify disproportionate responses which escalate the violence.

12 *AVOID* demonising adjectives such as "vicious," "cruel," "brutal," and "barbaric." These always describe one party's view of

what another party has done. To use them puts the journalist on that side and helps to justify an escalation of violence. *INSTEAD* report what you know about the wrongdoing and give as much information as you can about the reliability of other people's reports or descriptions of it. If it is still being investigated, say so, as a caution that the truth may not yet be known.

13 *AVOID* demonising labels such as "terrorist," "extremist," "fanatic," and "fundamentalist." These are always given by "us" to "them." No one ever uses them to describe himself or herself. And they are difficult, if not impossible, to apply impartially in every instance where they would be warranted. (What, for instance, is a "fundamentalist regime"? A working definition might be—an unelected government with leaders avowedly guided by religious belief. But many journalists would find it very difficult, in practice, so to describe the Bush administration, appointed to power by the US Supreme Court, in 2000, despite garnering half a million fewer votes than the Democrat, Al Gore.) In practice, therefore, to use such labels is always to take sides. They also generally mean the people labelled are unreasonable, which weakens the case for reasoning (negotiating) with them. *INSTEAD* try calling people by the names they give themselves. Or be more precise in your descriptions—for example, "bombers" and, for the attacks of September 11th, "suicide hijackers" are both less partisan and give more information than "terrorists."

14 *AVOID* focusing exclusively on the human rights abuses, misdemeanours, and wrongdoings on only one side. *INSTEAD* try to name ALL wrongdoers and treat allegations made by all parties in a conflict equally seriously. This means, not taking at face value but instead making equal efforts to establish whether any evidence exists to back them up, treating the victims with equal respect and the finding and punishing of all wrongdoers as being of equal importance.

15 *AVOID* making an opinion or claim seem like an established fact. This is how propaganda works—for example, the campaign, primarily aimed at US and UK media, to link Saddam Hussein to "international terrorism" in early 2002. Under a headline linking Iraq to the Taliban and Al Qaeda, came the claim that "Iraqi military intelligence officers are said to be assisting extreme Palestinian groups in attacks on Israel ...." "Said to be" obscures the question of who is doing the saying. See also "thought to be," "it's being seen as," and so on. *INSTEAD* tell your readers or your audience who said what. That way you avoid implicitly signing

up yourself and your news service to the allegations made by one party in the conflict against another.

16   *AVOID* greeting the signing of documents by leaders which bring about military victory or a ceasefire as necessarily creating peace. *INSTEAD* try to report on the issues which remain and on the needs and interests of those affected. What has to happen in order to remove incentives for further acts of violence? Ask what is being done to strengthen the means on the ground to handle and resolve conflict non-violently, to address development or structural needs in the society and to create a culture of peace?

17   *AVOID* waiting for leaders on "our" side to suggest or offer solutions. *INSTEAD* pick up and explore peace initiatives wherever they come from. Ask questions of politicians—for example, about ideas put forward by grass-roots organisations. Assess peace perspectives against what you know about the issues the parties are really trying to address; do not simply ignore them because they do not coincide with established positions. Include images of a solution, however partial or fragmentary—they may help to stimulate dialogue.

9 Conclusion

Towards a proactive approach to reporting African elections

As I was rounding off the manuscript for this book, Nic Cheeseman and Brian Klass co-authored a ground-breaking book titled *How to Rig an Election*.[1] The book critically examines the dynamics of global election rigging and how dictators and their accomplice have succeeded in earning vital goodwill points, while subtly perpetuating tyranny and dictatorship. They listed six ways in which dictators strategically plan ahead to win elections, thereby resulting in incumbents winning elections globally, seven times out of ten since the early 1990s. They asked a very important question in their book and somewhat also provided the answer:

> How is it possible that the flourishing of elections has coincided with a decade of democratic decline? The answer is that dictators, despots and counterfeit democrats have figured out how to rig elections and get away with it. An increasing number if authoritarian leaders are contesting multiparty elections, but are unwilling to put their fate in the hands of voters; in other words, more elections are being held, but more elections are also being rigged.[2]
>
> (p. 3)

The authors listed six ways through which elections are strategically rigged, they are as follows:

i   Invisible rigging: How to steal an election without being caught;
ii Buying hearts and minds: The art of electoral bribery;
iii Divide and rule: Violence as a political strategy;
iv Hack the election: Fake news and digital frontier;
v   Ballot-box stuffing: The last resort;
vi Potemkin: How to fool the West.

As I was gradually rounding off the manuscript for this book, I found myself asking the question: What role(s) can the media play in nipping these rigging strategies in the bud? How can journalists adopt a Peace Journalism approach towards proactively stemming electoral rigging and manipulations, which sometimes foster violence? The media is (should be) actively involved in the electoral process, from start to finish, and it should not be reactive in its reportage of the process, but it should also be proactive in informing and educating the public exhaustively, so that they can make informed electoral decisions, and so that they would be able to decipher when a government is attempting to rig and election.

1   Uncovering attempts at invincible rigging.

Cheeseman and Klass aver that the best way to rig an election is to do so before the ballots have even been printed. I argue that the best way for journalists expose plans for electoral rigging is long before ballots have been printed. They aver that dictators or counterfeit democrats use tactics such as gerrymandering, which allows those in power determine the boundary of the seats that opponents contest, resulting in many geographical blocks resembling "inkblots" rather than coherent geographical groupings. Gerrymandering is extremely useful in countries with a parliamentary system of government in which the party with the most seats earns the right to form the government. It was used effectively during the heydays of the government of Robert Mugabe in Zimbabwe. One of the reasons why gerrymandering has succeeded in countries where they have been used is because journalists do not seem to care or pay much attention to the system.

Another way through invisible rigging is fostered is through political exclusion. In many countries, incumbents and/or dictators formulate laws and draconian edicts that systematically exclude candidates and indeed the general public from contesting or voter in elections. Incumbents often "create" laws that make it impossible for certain members of the public to participate in the electoral process, and they also initiate laws that systematically neutralise prospective challengers, thereby making the coast clearer for themselves and their parties.

Journalists can make such issues an agenda for public discourse, thereby exposing the plans of the government intending to use them as strategy. Journalists can curtail gerrymandering and political exclusions by going the extra miles in exposing the background conditions under which elections occur as a reason to question their outcome. When the public are fully aware of the entire conditions under which elections occur, they would be able to question actions or policies of government that are capable of disenfranchising them.

2   Exposing the art (and act) of electoral bribery

In most African countries, winning elections requires giving handouts to voters. This explains why elections in Africa are some of the most expensive to organise in the world. Only a fraction of what is budgeted by the government actually goes into organising the elections, most of the money budgeted goes into "oiling the palms" of potential voters or their perceived influencers. This form of clientelism requires that when cash changes hands, votes are expected to follow. In Kenya, Nigeria, Ghana, Zimbabwe, and many other parts of Africa, incumbents who have access to state funds, "buy" votes, and sometimes go a step further to ensure that what they paid for is what they get. Although it is vital to state that vote buying does not always have the desired effect as individuals or groups may collect the money and vote conscientiously, it is nonetheless prevalent on the continent. According to Cheeseman and Klass,

> In the vast majority of countries, it is against the electoral rules to bribe voters by giving them gifts, or treat voters by handing out food and drink. However, most countries—particularly authoritarian states and counterfeit democracies do not enforce these basic electoral regulations. In turn, this creates an incentive for candidates from all parties to hand out small gifts to encourage voters to back their campaigns.

Journalists can help stem this unfortunate act by highlighting its negative impact on democracy to the members of the society. The impact of vote buying on democracy is immense. One of the most visible impacts is that it drives up the cost of elections, thereby making the entire process an exclusive preserve of the rich or those with access to state funds. Although Cheeseman and Klass argue that voter education have limited effect on whether or not the populace would accept bribes, it nonetheless can be a means through which journalists covering elections can help stem the process. By enlightening the public on the constitutional aspect of vote buying and its general socio-economic and sociopolitical impact, they can help to gradually build a critical mass of individuals who would reject selling their votes for stipends. Journalists can also highlight to the public instances where vote buying is rendered less effective either because opposition to the ruling regime is so intense that voters cannot be bribed. That way, they show that not everyone is doing it as the government would like to make them believe.

3   Exposing attempts at using violence as a political strategy

Political violence has been used as a political strategy for many years in most African elections, to the extent that the populace almost instinctively expect elections to be violent. Cheeseman and Klass aver that incumbents and authoritarian leaders are likely to use violence as a political strategy under two conditions. First, incumbents are far more likely to deploy violence when they operate in weak political systems and believe that they might actually lose. Second, state repression is more likely when the government believes that it can get away with it because it has powerful international backings. Authoritarian leaders use violence as a political strategy by removing rivals, for example, throwing them in jails, creating a culture of fear, and moving the masses by sometimes instigating ethno-religious clashes that lead to the displacement of thousands. Like previously stated in this book, not reporting, or under-reporting political violence is not Peace Journalism, the public depend very significantly on the media for up-to-date and precise coverage of violence where and when they occur, without demonising or finger-pointing, and with adequate contextualisation and backgrounding so that the public can fully understand what is at stake, as well as the various actors involved.

4   Countering and uncovering fake news and the digital frontier

The advent of the social media has provided authoritarian leaders and counterfeit democrats new avenues for systematically rigging elections. In Africa, for example, the social media has assumed very important significance as many people now have access to the Internet, many of them young people below the age of 30. Incumbents desirous of rigging elections see this as an advantage because this type of rigging is often difficult to track, since hacking and misinformation disseminated online are often anonymously carried out. According to Cheeseman and Klass, "hacking from the shadows makes it easier for authoritarian leaders to orchestrate rigging and then wash their hands [of] it and point the finger elsewhere."

Although social media sites have responded to the tendency for fake news to be disseminated through their platforms, by initiating a range of strategies designed to expose biased information and to prevent it from been circulated, the onus still lies with the journalist to present a balanced and more nuanced interpretation and contexts to societal happenings so that members of the public will easily decipher misinformation and/or subtle deceptions.

5   "Unstuffing" the ballot box

One of the most common ways through which elections are rigged in Africa is through the stuffing of ballot boxes. In fact, the post-electoral violence that rocked the nation of Kenya in 2007 was partly due to allegations of ballot-box stuffing by both the incumbent, Mwai Kibaki, and the opposition leader, Raila Odinga. Cheeseman and Klass are of the opinion that by the time Election Day arrives, there are four main rigging options available to both incumbents and the opposition. During voting, candidates can employ multiple voting and illegitimate voting. The other two strategies come into play once voting has taken place and are to stuff the ballot boxes with fake votes or to make sure the final result does not reflect the actual ballots cast by tampering with the counting process. This is a common feature in many elections on the continent of Africa.

While it is imprudent to adduce the responsibilities of stemming ballot-box stuffing to journalistic reportage, the media can nonetheless play active roles in stemming the trend. The authors propose a solution that involves international observer groups to conduct a parallel vote tabulation (PVT), which typically involves collecting results from a sample of polling stations in order to deter rigging during the counting process. I will further suggest that journalists should also endeavour to provide coverage of the activities of observer groups so that the public will be aware of the parallel result, which would help them note rigging when the differences are very obvious. Although PVT is not without its limitations, it is still one of the most effective ways through which rigging can be curbed.

6   Exposing attempts to "fool the West"

One of the ways dictators and counterfeit democrats rig elections is by carrying out so subtly that they not only get away with it, but they also fool the West in the process. This strategy has succeeded in part due to the desire of countries in the West who fund election observation and whose opinion on the legitimacy of the electoral process is taken seriously and highly sought after by authoritarian regimes and counterfeit democrats. What this means is that leaders whose countries are insulated from international pressures— either because they have economic and political ties to Western states or because of their resources and location.

Journalists must look beyond legitimacy as put forward by international observer groups and foreign governments and instead present the true account of what transpired in the election through detailed reportage that is devoid of bias. It is important for journalists to note that because an election was certified free and fair by international observers does not mean that it is free and fair indeed. They must look into other unspoken dynamics and power relations involved in the election, as well as the interests of individuals and groups that are protected through such blanket approvals of election results and processes.

Notes

1 Cheeseman, N. and Klass, B. 2018. *How to Rig and Election*. New Haven, CT: Yale University Press, 56.
2 Ibid.

Index

Printed in the United States
by Baker & Taylor Publisher Services